JOHN ADAMS
Public Servant

JOHN ADAMS
Public Servant

Bonnie L. Lukes

MORGAN
REYNOLDS
Incorporated

620 South Elm Street Suite 384
Greensboro, North Carolina 27406
http://www.morganreynolds.com

JOHN ADAMS: PUBLIC SERVANT

Picture Credits: *Courtesy of the Library of Congress*

Library of Congress Cataloging-in-Publication Data

Lukes, Bonnie L.
  John Adams: public servant / Bonnie L. Lukes.-- 1st ed.
    p.cm.
  Includes bibliographical references and index.
  ISBN 1-883846-80-3 (lib. bdg.)
    1. Adams, John, 1735-1826--Juvenile literature. 2. Presidents--United
States--Biography--Juvenile literature. [1. Adams, John, 1735-1826. 2. Presidents.] I.
Title.

E322 .L84 2000
973.4'4'092--dc21
[B]

00-060542

Printed in the United States of America
First Edition

For Max, last but worth the wait.

Contents

John Adams

Chapter One

"What Would You Do Child?"

It was not easy being John Adams. He worried about everything: the state of the world, the health of his cows, the way he walked, even the way he laughed. In private he doubted and questioned himself, but in public he frequently alienated people with a self-righteous and egotistical attitude. He yearned for fame, but he was ashamed of his eagerness to achieve it. He was a warm and sensuous person with a zest for life, yet he often appeared cold and forbidding. He tried always to do the right thing, but he was never certain that he had. He was a witty man, but the wit was sometimes too sharp and caused hurt feelings. "Oh!" he lamented to his diary, "that I could . . . acquire that meekness, and humility, which are the sure marks . . . of a great and generous Soul . . . "

John Adams was born in the village of Braintree (later called Quincy) in the colony of Massachusetts on October 30, 1735. John Adams Sr.—known as Deacon—could not have guessed his firstborn child would participate in a revolution that would change the world. And he would have been outraged if anyone had suggested that the thirteen American colonies might separate from England and start a new nation. Surely, the British Empire was the most powerful in the entire world, and he and his newborn son proud subjects of its king. Nothing could change that. Braintree, which lay ten miles south of Boston, was still awash with the stern spirit of its Puritan founders. Protestant Christianity dominated, and the town's spiritual and social activities centered around the meetinghouse. Every Sunday the whole town gathered for the two church services—one in the morning and one in the evening. John's sense of self would always be intertwined with his Puritan upbringing, and his belief in God and the Bible.

Deacon Adams was a respected man in Braintree. He had married Susanna Boylston—daughter of one of the most prominent families in Massachusetts. Deacon and Susanna had two more children after John: Peter and Elihu. Although Deacon worked hard as a farmer and a shoemaker, he could not afford to send all three children to college. As the eldest, John would be the one to be educated. They planned for him to attend Harvard College in Cambridge and study for the ministry.

At age six John began his formal education at Dame Belcher's primary school. Dame Belcher held school in her house and taught reading, writing and simple arithmetic. John's first primer combined learning the alphabet with lessons in morality. The children recited in unison such rhymes as "In Adam's Fall, We Sinned all," and "The Idle Fool is whipt at school."

John soon outgrew Mrs. Belcher's school. Because his parents had destined him for the ministry, he was then enrolled in Braintree's Latin School rather than in public school. Students attended the Latin School for six to eight years, or until the schoolmaster judged them capable of passing Harvard's entrance examination.

Unfortunately, John disliked school and had little interest in learning. He loved the outdoors and especially enjoyed hunting and fishing. He learned how to use a gun by the time he was nine, and he often skipped school to go hunting for crows and squirrels. The marsh, where he could shoot wild fowl and swim, was his favorite spot. He could spend a whole day there without food, lying on the cold ground waiting for the birds to appear. "I cared not what I did," he said, "if I could but get away from school."

It was not lost on Deacon Adams that his son preferred hunting to learning. When questioned, John explained that he did not like books, and he did not want to go to college.

"What would you do Child?" his father asked.

"Be a Farmer," John replied.

"A Farmer? Well I will shew you what it is to be a Farmer. You shall go with me to Penny ferry tomorrow Morning and help me get Thatch."

The next day John and his father worked all day in the marsh up to their knees in mud, hacking and tying the thatch into bundles. It was a long, exhausting day. But the next morning when Deacon Adams asked his son how he had liked being a farmer, John was too stubborn to admit to sore and aching muscles. Instead, he answered, "I like it very well, Sir."

"Ay," the deacon answered, "but I don't like it so well: so you shall go to School to day."

John returned to school, but his unhappiness grew. He detested his teacher, Joseph Cleverly, whom he would later describe as "the most indolent [lazy] Man I ever knew." Finally, at age fifteen, John again approached his father about being a farmer. Deacon Adams explained that he had his heart set on his oldest son going to college and asked why John did not want to fulfill this dream. John answered honestly. "Sir I don't like my Schoolmaster. He is so negligent and so cross that I never can learn any thing under him. If you will be so good as to perswade Mr. Marsh to take me, I will apply myself to my Studies . . . and go to Colledge as soon as I can be prepared."

Joseph Marsh ran a private boarding school just two houses away, and Deacon Adams made arrangements with him that same evening. Marsh was a kind and patient teacher, and John flourished under his instruction. For the first time, he began to take his studies seriously. Within a year, Marsh declared him ready for Harvard.

Early on the day of Harvard's entrance examinations,

John rode his horse to Mr. Marsh's house. He dreaded the exams, but it soothed his mind to know that Marsh was accompanying him. However, when he reached Marsh's house, he found his teacher ill and unable to travel. John would have to go alone. Unnerved, he first thought he would turn around and go back home. But he could not bear to disappoint either his father or his teacher.

Joseph Marsh assured him that he would have no difficulty with the examination. John was not so certain. "I had not the same confidence in myself, and suffered a very mancholly Journey," he later recalled.

In 1751, Harvard had four teachers, called tutors. Each tutor was assigned one class, which he kept throughout its entire four years of study. If John were admitted to Harvard, his tutor would be Joseph Mayhew. Consequently, it was Mayhew who tested him on Latin, the exam he dreaded most.

Mayhew handed him a long paragraph to be translated from English to Latin. With a sinking heart, John saw he did not know the Latin translation for many of the English words. "Thinking that I must translate it without a dictionary," Adams later wrote, "I was in a great fright and expected to be [refused admission], an Event that I dreaded above all things." But the tutor handed him a dictionary and told him to take his time. John breathed a sigh of relief, completed the translation, and was "declared admitted."

In the fall of 1751, at age sixteen, John began his

studies at Harvard. The schedule was demanding, but he soon "perceived a growing Curiosity, a Love of Books and a fondness for Study," he had never before experienced. He said that this new thirst for learning diverted him from the sport of hunting and even lessened his desire for the "Society of the Ladies."

In his third year at Harvard something happened that would affect the whole course of his life. He accepted an invitation to join a newly formed campus club that devoted evenings to reading aloud newly published essays, poetry or plays. John was often chosen to read, and soon it was noted that he had a flair for public speaking. Friends began suggesting that he would "make a better Lawyer than [a clergyman]."

For the first time, he considered studying law. But such a decision would present difficulties. One problem was finances. "I had no Money," he wrote, "and my Father having three Sons, had done as much for me, in the Expences of my Education as his ... Circumstances could justify and as my . . . honor would allow me to ask."

Moreover, the legal profession itself posed a problem. In some circles, practicing law was not yet considered a respectable occupation. Further, as a devout Christian, John questioned his own motives. He knew he wanted to practice law because the profession offered a chance for fame and fortune, and he thought these were inappropriate reasons. Yet, he knew he did not have a personality suited to the ministry. He was too blunt, too impatient.

He finally decided to teach school for a few years while he made up his mind.

In August 1755, just three weeks after graduation, John began teaching in Worcester, a town located sixty miles from Braintree. He was not yet twenty. Adams did not enjoy teaching. In a letter to a former college classmate, he described his students as "a large number of little runtlings, just capable of lisping A B C, and [of] troubling the master."

Furthermore, Worcester itself, was a frontier town that had none of the urban sophistication John had experienced while at Harvard. He knew he could never achieve the fame he craved in such a backwoods town. "I have no Books, no Time, no Friends. I must therefore be contented to live and die an ignorant, obscure fellow," he complained in his diary.

As the end of his first year of teaching neared, Adams remained torn between law and the ministry. His strong Puritan conscience urged him toward the ministry, but his Puritan common sense told him the law. Such indecisiveness led to procrastination. Entry after entry in his diary reflected dissatisfaction with himself for wasting time. "Dreamed away the Time," he wrote again and again. He would then determine to do better. "I am resolved to rise with the Sun . . ." he wrote on July 21, 1756. "I will stand collected within my self and think upon what I read and what I see. I will strive with all my soul to be something more than Persons who have had less Advantages than myself." But the next day he wrote in disgust: "Rose not till 7 o clock. This is the usual Fate of my Resolutions!"

During this difficult period, the name of James Putnam, an attorney in Worcester, increasingly appeared in John's diary. And on Sunday, August 22, 1756, Adams noted in his diary: "Yesterday I compleated a Contract with Mr. Putnam, to study Law under his Inspection for two years." Lingering pangs of conscience over rejecting the ministry compelled him to add: "I set out with firm Resolutions . . . never to commit any meanness or injustice in the Practice of Law."

Chapter Two

Law and Love

Adams agreed to pay Putnam one hundred dollars for tutoring services—an amount he had saved from his previous year's teaching salary. But he must also pay for food and lodging. Unwilling to burden his father with further expense, he continued in his job as schoolmaster because the salary included payment of room and board. Then followed two grueling years of teaching during the day, studying law at night, and attending court sessions with Putnam. But in the fall of 1758, John completed his training.

Friends urged him to remain in Worcester, but he did not want to begin a law career in competition with his teacher. He decided to return to his hometown of Braintree, which had no practicing attorney. And more importantly, Braintree was in the Boston judicial district. Adams knew that if he wanted recognition, Boston was the place to achieve it. Before he could practice law, however, he must be admitted to the Massachusetts bar.

On October 4, John returned to his parents' home in Braintree. Three weeks later, he rode into Boston to seek admission to the bar. To be accepted, he needed a respected lawyer to sponsor him. The first day in the city, he did nothing but observe court proceedings. Being in the presence of so many prominent attorneys left him awestruck, and he fought a growing sense of inadequacy. "I had no Acquaintance with any Body but [Robert Treat] Paine and [Samuel] Quincy," he noted in his diary, "and they took but little Notice [of me]." Unlike other aspiring lawyers his age—Samuel Quincy, for example—Adams could not depend on influential family connections. "It is my Destiny," he lamented in his diary, "to dig Treasures with my own fingers. No Body will lend me or sell me a Pick axe."

The next morning, scared but determined, John went to see Jeremiah Gridley, the dean of Massachusetts's lawyers. After questioning John extensively, Gridley was so impressed that he promised to serve as his sponsor, and offered to lend him whatever law books he needed. John had not only found a sponsor, he had snared the best one available.

On Monday, November 6, 1758, both John and Sam Quincy were to be presented to the court. John, nervous and apprehensive, wanted to ensure that Gridley remembered his promise. He went twice to Gridley's office only to be told that the attorney had not yet arrived. Finally, John went alone to the courtroom, where he waited with growing anxiety. The noon hour passed and still no Gridley. John fretted that the well-connected Sam Quincy would be accepted, and he himself would not. Shortly after noon, however, Jeremiah Gridley sauntered into the courtroom. He conferred briefly with the other lawyers, then rose and recommended both John and Sam to the court. For John, it was the end of one journey and the beginning of another.

Most of the lawsuits in Braintree had to do with straying livestock, and Adams's first case was no exception. It involved a stray horse, and Adams, young and inexperienced, lost the case on a technicality. The client was angry, and John feared public ridicule over the defeat. He worried that he would never get another client. "It will be said, [that] I undertook the Case but was unable to manage it."

People in Braintree were quick to sue, however, and Adams soon acquired other clients. He won some cases, but the suits all involved trivial issues that did little to enhance a lawyer's reputation. Confident that he would eventually try more important cases, John now sought social camaraderie and relaxation among a wide circle of young men and women in Braintree. They gathered often to play cards, engage in sing-a-longs, and share their dreams for the future.

John's closest friend in Braintree was Richard Cranch, an established businessman. They would remain devoted friends throughout their lifetimes—despite the fact that both of them fell under the spell of Hannah Quincy—Braintree's most popular young maiden.

It was during his first year of practicing law that John fell in love with the flirtatious Hannah Quincy. Few young men in Braintree escaped Hannah's wiles, but John fell especially hard. Soon he could not concentrate on his work. "My mind is liable to be called off from Law, by a Girl . . . a Poem, a Love Letter . . ."

John was crushed when the lovely Hannah suddenly married someone else. He shared his anguish with Cranch: "If I look upon a Law Book and labor to exert all my Attention, my Eyes tis true are on the Book, but Imagination is at a Tea Table with [Hannah], seeing That Face, those Eyes, that Shape, that familiar friendly look . . . I go to bed and . . . dream about the same . . ."

Time passed, however, and John's wounded pride began to heal. By 1761, Cranch was courting Mary Smith, the oldest of Reverend William Smith's three daughters. He convinced John to accompany him to the Smith parsonage in Weymouth, four miles from Braintree. John had met Abigail Smith two years earlier, when she was only fifteen. Now he discovered that the girl he met earlier had matured into a lovely, young woman. John, at age twenty-six, was nine years older than Abigail, but the attraction between them at this second meeting was strong and immediate.

Abigail, like most women at that time, had been denied a formal education, but her father taught her to read and

John Adams fell in love with charming Abigail Smith.

write and encouraged a love of books. She had her own opinions and did not hesitate to express them. She knew how to make John laugh at himself, and she was feisty enough to deal with his sometimes critical attitude.

In May of 1761—the same year John and Abigail fell in love—John's father died, a victim of an influenza epidemic that swept through Braintree. The deacon's will divided his property among his wife and sons. Because John had been the one to receive an education, he inherited the smallest share—the farmhouse a few yards from the home in which he was born, ten acres of adjoining land, and thirty additional acres elsewhere in Braintree.

By November, Adams had completed three years of practice in the Lower Court. This earned him the right to try cases in Superior Court, where he would encounter more challenging issues. Superior Court lawyers "rode the circuit," moving from county to county as the court itself moved. This meant John and Abigail were apart for weeks at a time. Letters flew back and forth between them.

In one, Abigail asked John to make a list of her faults, and John who never hesitated to correct anyone, was happy to do so. He listed six that ranged from her indifferent card playing to her untrained singing voice to her habit of "sitting with the Leggs [crossed]." Far from being devastated, Abigail thanked him for the list and saucily added that "a gentleman has no business to concern himself about the Leggs of a Lady. . . ."

Later, a humbler Adams wrote: "O my dear Girl, I thank Heaven that another Fortnight will restore you to me— after so long a separation. My soul and Body have both been thrown in to Disorder, by your Absence . . . I see nothing but Faults, Follies, Frailties and Defects in any Body, lately."

Despite daily letters, the separations grew harder to bear as their courtship grew increasingly passionate— even giddy. On one of John's visits to Abigail, he carried a letter which demanded that she "give [the bearer] as many Kisses . . . as he shall please to demand and charge them to my Account."

They were married on October 25, 1764. He was twenty-nine, she was nineteen. They began their life together in the gray, weatherbeaten farmhouse John inherited from his father. John had already set up his law office and library on the ground floor, which also contained the large kitchen, a parlor, and a tiny room for the family servant. Four bedrooms occupied the top floor, two of them tiny cubbyholes under the eaves.

Abigail stabilized John's life and gave him a long-sought inner peace. He became more patient with himself and with others. She also instilled in him a new self-confidence. This had become evident even a year before their marriage when he overcame his ingrained fear of public ridicule and wrote a series of political essays for the *Boston Gazette.*

By the time John and Abigail married, John's hard

work and growing self-discipline had begun to bear fruit. His law practice was doing well, and the published essays had brought him a measure of recognition in Boston. And now he had Abigail by his side. At Christmas, she told John he would become a father in the summer. It must have seemed to the young couple that the future could never surpass the present in excitement or surprises. But a great drama lay ahead, one that neither John nor Abigail could have envisioned.

Chapter Three

Rallying to the Cause

In 1760, four years before John and Abigail married, George III became king. England, at the time, was involved in the French and Indian War—much of which was fought on American soil. Adams served in the war only briefly, acting as a courier. But like most colonists, he took pride in the part Americans played in England's victory.

The war ended in 1765 and left England burdened with a huge national debt. Deciding that the American colonies should help pay the debt, Parliament proposed a stamp tax. Americans reacted angrily, charging that this was taxation without representation because they had no representatives in Parliament. Petitions of protest went unanswered, but the colonists persisted.

In Boston, John Adams's cousin Sam Adams organized a secret group that would be called the Sons of Liberty. When certain merchants organized a boycott on British imports, the Sons of Liberty used intimidation and threats to ensure that *all* merchants cooperated.

The Stamp Act crisis divided Americans into two opposing camps: Loyalists and patriots. Loyalists, as the name implies, were loyal to the British empire and believed that colonists should support all government policies. Patriots fiercely guarded colonial rights and liberties and advocated limiting the power of the king.

As a patriot, Adams opposed the Stamp Act because he considered it unconstitutional. But his involvement in the stamp rebellion developed slowly. He was torn over how to actively participate in the protest. He was not an extremist like his cousin Sam, and he abhorred mob violence. He also recognized that the courts had to obey the king. If angry Bostonians made it impossible to distribute the stamps, the courts would close and Adams would lose his source of income. The fear of losing his livelihood was magnified by the impending birth of his first child.

Circuit riding still kept him away from home for long periods—even during Abigail's pregnancy. Abigail was fond of her mother-in-law who lived next door, but she wanted to be with her own mother during childbirth. When the time drew near, Abigail returned to her parents' house in Weymouth. There, on July 14, 1765, she gave birth to a daughter. The baby was named Abigail after her mother, but she would always be called Nabby.

In the meantime, despite colonial boycotts and appeals to the king, the Stamp Act became official on November 1, 1765. However, Lieutenant-Governor Thomas Hutchinson

Samuel Adams led the patriotic group, the Sons of Liberty.

feared that bringing the stamps into Boston would cause a full-scale riot. So the stamps were not distributed but kept at Castle William, a fortress on an island in Boston harbor. With the stamps unavailable, business activities ground to a halt. The Boston port closed, and the courts suspended business.

Now Adams had an unusual amount of leisure time. He continued to read and study, and publish articles, but mainly he pondered over the Stamp Act. Entry after entry in his diary revealed his pre-occupation. "At Home, with my family. Thinking." And again, "At Home. Thinking, reading, searching, concerning Taxation without consent . . ."

His rising enthusiasm for what he called "the Cause," is apparent in a diary entry made December 18. "The Year 1765 has been the most remarkable Year of my Life. That enormous Engine, fabricated by the British Parliament, for battering down all the Rights and Liberties of America, I mean the Stamp Act, has raised and spread, [through] the whole Continent, a Spirit that will be recorded to our Honor . . . The people have become more . . . determined to defend [their liberties] than they were ever before . . ."

On a personal level, Adams resented the Stamp Act because he feared his involvement would undo everything he had thus far accomplished. "I have had Poverty to struggle with . . . [and] few to assist me," he wrote, "so that I have groped in dark Obscurity, till of late, and had but just . . . gained a small degree of Reputation, when this [wretched] Project was set on foot for my Ruin . . ."

But the people of Braintree were apparently impressed with his resistance to the Stamp Act. At a town meeting on March 3, 1766, they elected him one of the town's selectmen. Adams wrote in his diary: "It gave me much pleasure to find I had so many Friends, and that my Conduct in Town [Boston], has been not disapproved." Adams had not campaigned for the office. "The Choice was quite unexpected to me," he said.

Ultimately, England repealed the Stamp Act; the courts reopened in April; and Adams resumed practicing law. He ignored politics and devoted his time to his thriving law practice, his selectman duties, and his small farm. The farm was not profitable, but Adams found peace and serenity there. All his life, the Braintree farm would serve as a refuge from the world, "a place with fields to walk and hills to climb."

By late 1766, Abigail was pregnant for the second time. Once again, she went to her parents' home, where she gave birth to her first son on July 11, 1767. The sturdy, healthy boy was named John Quincy after his maternal great-grandfather.

As Adams's practice grew, he spent more and more time in Boston away from Abigail and the children. He was exhilarated by the town's intellectual atmosphere and attracted to the financial opportunities it offered. Before long, Adams decided to move his family there.

He did not make that decision lightly. As usual, he questioned his motives: "Am I grasping at Money, or

Scheming for Power?" But in April 1768, he declined re-election to his selectman post in Braintree and moved his family—Abigail, the baby Johnny, and Nabby, not quite three years old—to a house on Brattle Square in Boston.

Moving from tiny Braintree to a city with over 18,000 people required some adjusting. The noise alone was disconcerting. Bustling, busy people crowded the streets; and boisterous sailors roamed the city until late at night. Church bells—which seemed to Abigail to ring continuously—tolled the news of funerals, fires, or civil disturbances, and summoned people to the Meeting House for church services.

The Adams home attracted an assortment of visitors. John's long-time close friend, Jonathan Sewall visited. Now a Loyalist, Jonathan was the Chief prosecutor for the Crown. Dr. Joseph Warren, a staunch patriot and friend, stopped by often as did Sam Adams and the wealthy John Hancock—a behind-the-scenes supporter of the Sons of Liberty. Discussions often centered around politics.

The political tumult in Boston subsided following the repeal of the Stamp Act. But, then, Parliament passed the Townshend Acts, laws which imposed a customs duty on products like tea and glass. Customs Commissioners arrived from England with search warrants that allowed them to enter homes and shops to look for smuggled goods. And on June 1768, they seized John Hancock's sloop *Liberty* on the charge that it had been used to smuggle wine ashore. Angered by what they saw as a trumped-up charge, a Boston crowd mobbed the agents, forcing them to flee for their lives.

Once again the city was in turmoil, and Adams could not avoid being caught up in the swirl of events. He was asked to defend Hancock against the smuggling charges— a case that pitted him against his friend Sewall. Adams described the Hancock case as "a painfull Drudgery," because it dragged on throughout the entire winter. Finally in March of 1769, Adams's successful defense coupled with a lack of evidence forced the prosecution to withdraw the suit.

At some point during the trial, Jonathan Sewall dined with John and Abigail. "This was always . . . acceptable . . .," Adams wrote later, "for although We were at [odds] in Politicks We had never . . . cooled in the Warmth of our Friendship." After dinner when the two men were alone, Sewall confessed that he had come to urge Adams to succeed him as the Crown's chief legal officer. Thomas Hutchinson, now the acting governor, had decided that Adams "was the best entitled to the Office," Sewall said.

Adams knew that accepting this offer would ensure his success. It was, he wrote, "a sure introduction to the most profitable Business in the Province and . . . a first Step in the Ladder of Royal Favour and promotion." Nevertheless, he turned down the offer "in an instant," unwilling to put himself "under any . . . Obligations of Gratitude to the Government for any of their favours." It could not have been easy for him to turn his back on a chance for wealth and recognition, but it would not be the last time he did so. Throughout his life, Adams refused to compromise his principles for the sake of personal gain.

Meanwhile shortly after the Hancock incident, England dispatched four regiments of soldiers to bring the unruly Bostonians into submission. The warships had anchored in Boston Harbor with guns aimed at the town. Adams, off riding circuit, missed the troops' arrival.

"On my return," he later wrote, "I found . . . Boston full of Troops . . . Through the whole succeeding fall and Winter a Regiment was exercised . . . directly in Front of my house . . . Their very Appearance in Boston was . . . proof to me, that the determination [of] Great Britain to subjugate [enslave] Us, was too deep . . . ever to be altered by Us."

Now Adams became increasingly involved in politics. Along with others, he advised against appropriating money to feed and house the British troops. He supported the Sons of Liberty by writing occasional propaganda treatises for them. However, he still deplored the group's often violent and destructive methods of protest—what he called mob activities.

The year 1769 ended with the British soldiers still occupying Boston, and with a new baby in the Adams household. Susanna was born on December 28 in the house on Brattle Square—where Abigail now served coffee instead of tea because of a continuing boycott against English products.

Inside his home, surrounded by a loving wife and three children, Adams found peace. Outside, however, the voices grew increasingly shrill. British soldiers patrolling Boston streets were pursued by taunting children, who ridiculed their red uniforms by calling them Lobsterbacks or Bloodybacks. Fights and brawls broke out daily between citizens and soldiers. Tension covered Boston like a thick fog rolling in from the bay. And at Brattle Square, John and Abigail waited to see what would come next.

Chapter Four

In Search of Justice

At 8:00 P.M. on the evening of March 5, 1770, the violence—which had threatened since the arrival of the British troops—suddenly erupted. Fights between civilians and soldiers broke out all over Boston.

On King Street, near John Adams's home, a group of young apprentices taunted Private Hugh White, who stood guard in front of the Custom House. They pelted him with icy snowballs and dared him to fire on them. At the same time, angry civilians—fresh from violent encounters in other parts of town—converged on King Street. Private White, fearing for his life, shouted to the nearby main guard for help.

Captain Thomas Preston, the British officer of the day, led a squad of seven soldiers to White's rescue. The crowd had grown to well over 300 people. Preston tried to reason with them, but the enraged mob responded with curses, icy snowballs, and taunts to go ahead and shoot. In the confusion, someone shouted, "Fire!" Shots rang out, and when the smoke cleared two Bostonians lay dead in the snow; three were dying; six more had been wounded but would survive.

Meanwhile, John Adams, meeting with his lawyers' club on the other side of Boston, had heard church bells ringing across town. Thinking the bells meant fire, the members immediately disbanded to offer help. However, out in the street they discovered there was no fire. "We were informed that the British soldiers had fired on the Inhabitants, killed some and wounded others near the Town House," Adams later recalled.

John's first concern was for Abigail's safety; she was alone at home except for the children and one female servant. Only a month earlier, the baby Susanna—just thirteen months old—had died. "Little Suky," as John affectionately called her, had been frail since birth, and despite all of Dr. Warren's efforts, she failed to gain weight. Abigail had been too exhausted and overcome with grief to attend the burial service. Moreover, she was expecting another baby in May.

John hurried through Boston's ice-encrusted streets, paying no attention to the soldiers he encountered "with their Musquets all shouldered and their Bayonetts all fixed." To reach his front door, Adams had to squeeze past them, which he did "without taking the least notice of them, or they of me, any more than if they had been marble Statues."

Abigail had been frightened when she first heard the

screaming crowds and the gunfire so close to her home. But by the time John arrived, she was calm. They talked about the night's events and its possible consequences. Adams was upset over the town's mob violence, but he blamed the shootings on the British leaders who had sent troops to Boston in the first place.

In the predawn hours, long after John and Abigail slept, Governor Thomas Hutchinson issued warrants for the arrest of Captain Preston and the soldiers involved in the shootings. They would be tried for murder. But could they receive a fair trial? Would any lawyer in Boston be willing to defend them?

The morning after the shootings, John Adams agreed to represent Preston and the accused soldiers. He said later that he never hesitated because "Council ought to be the very last thing that an accused Person should [lack] in a free Country." It is also probable that Sam Adams encouraged him to take the case, because the patriots did not want it said that Preston and the soldiers did not receive a fair trial.

The soldiers asked to be tried with their captain, but at Adams's urging, the court ruled to try Preston and the soldiers separately. Governor Hutchinson delayed the trials until fall, in the hope that the anger of Boston citizens would cool during the interim.

Meanwhile, life was not uneventful for John and Abigail. On May 29, their second son Charles was born. And in June, the Boston Town Meeting elected John to the Massachusetts Assembly. His election meant he would be targeted by the British government as one of Boston's treasonous radicals—a dangerous position. Adams was not unaware of this." I could scarce perceive a possibility that I should ever . . . escape with my Life," he wrote.

Captain Preston's trial began October 24, 1770. The question before the jury was whether or not Preston had ordered his men to fire. Adams and his defense team called twenty-three witnesses who testified that the soldiers had been harassed and intimidated by the crowd. The prosecution called fifteen witnesses but could not prove that Preston had ordered his men to shoot. The jury took less than three hours to return with a "not guilty" verdict.

Three weeks later the soldiers were tried. There was no doubt that the soldiers had killed five Boston citizens, but Adams would try to show that they had fired because they feared for their lives. At the very least, he wanted to convince the jury that because of their endangerment, the soldiers were guilty of no more than manslaughter.

After two and one-half hours of deliberation, the jury found six of the eight soldiers not guilty. Two were judged "not guilty of murder, but guilty of manslaughter." Those two pled "benefit of clergy"—a device that could be used by first-time offenders to avoid punishment. They were freed after being branded on their thumbs.

The verdict was a great personal victory for Adams. He

later described his defense of the British soldiers as "one of the best Pieces of Service I ever rendered my Country." At the time, however, he believed that he had destroyed his chances for a political career.

The trials—combined with Adams's legislative duties, the demands of his law practice, and his family responsibilities—proved too much. In February 1771, he collapsed from physical and emotional exhaustion. Abigail's health was not robust either. Four pregnancies in six years had taken their toll. Adams decided it would be best for everyone to move his family back to Braintree.

On his first morning back at the farm, Adams wrote in his diary that from now on he would divide his time between farming and the law: "Farewell Politicks." But within sixteen months, he was restless and ready to return to the city. His health had improved, and Boston had been quiet for almost two years. The soldiers were gone, and the Townshend Acts which had caused such great unrest had been repealed. Only the tax on tea remained.

Adams, now thirty-seven years old, believed he had learned how to live in Boston without ruining his health. He would practice law, look after his family, and return to Braintree occasionally to relax and oversee farming activities. "Above all Things," he wrote, "I must avoid Politicks, Political Clubbs, Town Meetings, [and] General Court [the legislature] . . ."

In August 1772, Adams purchased a brick house on Queen Street near his law office. And for the fifth time in four years the family prepared to move, although Abigail was in the last weeks of another pregnancy. A third son, Thomas, was born at Braintree on September 15. In November, Abigail—still weak from childbirth—arrived on Queen Street with the children. Nabby was seven, John Quincy five, Charles two-and-a-half, and the baby Thomas only two months old. Abigail herself was now twenty-eight.

Despite his sincere intentions, the family had scarcely settled in before Adams was again involved in Boston politics. England had passed a new law ordering that salaries of Massachusetts judges be paid by the Crown rather than by the colonial assembly. Adams believed this law would destroy the colony's judicial independence, and he said so in essays printed in the *Boston Gazette.*

In May 1773 Adams was elected to the Council, the upper house of the Assembly. Hutchinson, however, vetoed his selection. Adams seemed neither surprised nor perturbed by the veto. His diary entries that summer reveal an unusual serenity. He and Abigail enjoyed trips to the farm, attended a wedding, and visited relatives. Boston was quiet. The British soldiers were gone. Political rebellion appeared to have ended. Then on December 17, 1773, John informed his diary: "Last Night 3 Cargoes of Bohea Tea were emptied into the Sea."

The tea ships had arrived in Boston in November. Dockworkers refused to unload the tea because the Sons of Liberty had branded tea importers enemies of America.

Patriots wanted the tea sent back to England without paying the tax. But Governor Hutchinson denied the ships clearance to sail. Consequently, on the night of December 16, the Sons of Liberty had a tea party. Dressed as Mohawk Indians, they boarded the three British ships and calmly dumped forty-five tons of tea into Boston Harbor. No other part of the ships' cargo was touched.

John Adams—who believed that mobs could be justified only when constitutional liberties were at stake—was impressed by what came to be called the Boston Tea Party. "This is the most magnificent Movement of all," he wrote in his diary. "There is a Dignity . . . in this [latest] Effort of the Patriots, that I greatly admire . . . The People should never rise, without doing something to be remembered—something notable." Nevertheless, Adams knew England would be furious. "What Measures will the Ministry take, in Consequence of this? . . . Will they punish Us? How?" Five months passed before the answer came.

During that tense period, patriots stored five hundred barrels of gunpowder at Boston and Charleston. Militia companies were reinforced and new ones formed. But while Massachusetts prepared for the worst, Adams busied himself with a happier task. He wrote in his diary on February 28, 1774, that he had bought the house where he was born. "The Buildings and the Water, I wanted, very much. That beautifull, winding, meandering Brook, which runs thro this farm, always delighted me."

In May, Bostonians learned the consequences of destroying the tea. Parliament passed four laws meant to crush any further resistance in Massachusetts and serve as an example to the other colonies. These laws, which were promptly labeled the Intolerable Acts, closed Boston ports and gave the royal governor enormous new powers: he could even ban town meetings. And troops were again dispatched to Boston to ensure that the laws were enforced. Governor Hutchinson was recalled to England, and General Thomas Gage—the commander-in-chief of the British army in America—replaced him as governor.

Before the new governor could ban colonial meetings, the Massachusetts Assembly called for a continental congress—a meeting of representatives from all the colonies. Five delegates were elected to represent Massachusetts at the First Continental Congress, which would be held in Philadelphia. John Adams, off riding the eastern court circuit, was one of the five.

Chapter Five

"I Feel Myself Unequal to this Business"

When John Adams first learned about the Continental Congress, he called it "an assembly of the wisest Men upon the Continent . . ." Yet, typically, he questioned his own ability. "I feel myself unequal to this Business," he told Abigail. "A more extensive Knowledge . . . is necessary, than I am Master of."

The Massachusetts delegates began the 300-mile journey to Philadelphia on August 10, 1774. Adams was pleased with their reception along the way. In Connecticut, every town rang its bells and fired its cannons in salute. They were wined and dined as they progressed down through New Jersey and New York. Adams, who had never been outside of Massachusetts, delighted in these new experiences. He wrote Abigail from New Jersey: "We have had Opportunities to see the World, and to form Acquaintances with the most . . . famous men in the several colonies we have passed through."

They reached Philadelphia on August 29. On Monday, September 5, all of the delegates from the various states gathered informally at the City Tavern on Second Street. It was a diverse group—a mix of conservatives and moderates, as well as radicals like Sam Adams. The first issue was to decide where the Congress should meet. Carpenters' Hall was suggested, and the delegates walked over to inspect it. They liked the white-paneled room with its library and long hall where they could walk and engage in private conversations. In the first vote of the first Continental Congress, a large majority voted to use the Hall.

The delegates settled down to debate the critical issues facing the colonies. But they had scarcely begun when a messenger arrived with an alarming report that British soldiers had shelled Boston. The news threw both the Congress and the city into turmoil. John, overwhelmed with anxiety, wrote to Abigail: "When or where this Letter will find you, I know not. In what . . . Distress and Terror, I cannot foresee. We have received a confused Account . . . of a dreadfull Catastrophy . . . We are waiting with the Utmost Anxiety . . . for further [news]." To his great relief, word soon came that the report had been erroneous.

Before long the Congress began meeting in committees and subcommittees rather than in general sessions. Both John and Sam Adams served on these committees. They were careful, however, not to antagonize anyone because Massachusetts needed help. England had inflicted the punishing Intolerable Acts only on Massachusetts, and John remained uncertain of how much support could be expected from the other colonies. Then on September 16, Paul Revere arrived from Boston carrying the Suffolk Resolves.

The Resolves spoke directly and to the point: the Intolerable Acts were unconstitutional, and Massachusetts did not have to obey them. They also called for a boycott on all trade with England. These were the strongest statements yet made against England, but the delegates—even George Washington, the moderate from Virginia—endorsed the Resolves. Now John Adams had his answer. That night he wrote in his diary: "This was one of the happiest Days of my Life . . . This Day convinced me that America will support . . . Massachusetts or perish with her."

But his happiness was marred by the knowledge that in Boston General Gage was preparing the British soldiers for war. He worried about Abigail and how frightened she must be "amidst the Confusions and Dangers" around her. In a letter written September 29, he told her: "I long to return and administer all the consolation in my power . . ." Before ending the letter, however, he added that he would see the business of the Congress completed even if it meant remaining in Philadelphia until after Christmas.

But after seven intense weeks, the delegates hammered out a Declaration of Rights and agreed on an economic boycott they hoped would force Parliament to repeal the Intolerable Acts. The Congress adjourned on October 26, and the tired delegates happily headed home. They agreed to meet again in early May if necessary. That evening Adams wrote in his diary: "It is not very likely that I shall ever see this Part of the World again . . ."

He had been away from home for three months, and was eager to see Abigail and the children. But he scarcely had time to catch up on family news before he was elected to the Massachusetts assembly. That winter Adams also wrote a series of political essays for the *Boston Gazette* in which he defended colonial resistance to England. He was at work on one of these on April 19, 1775, when news came that the blood of colonial Americans had been spilled on the village green at Lexington.

General Gage had sent a large detail of British soldiers to seize the patriot weapons and gunpowder stored at Concord. But when the Redcoats reached Lexington, they found militiamen waiting for them. Shots were fired, and within minutes eight Americans lay dead.

The British continued on to Concord, but word of Lexington spread quickly, and Massachusetts militia-men—reinforced by other New Englanders—forced the British soldiers to fall back. A bloody retreat to Boston ensued. Patriots waited in fields along the road, shooting from behind walls. By the time the British reached Boston, 73 of their men had been killed and 174 wounded. American losses were much lower: 49 killed and 39 wounded. Moreover, the militia had the royal army blocked from re-entering the countryside. The British could leave Boston only by sea.

On April 22, Adams went on horseback to Cambridge

to talk with the officers of the ragged, makeshift American army. Then he continued on to Lexington to hear firsthand what had happened there. What the people told him effectively abolished any remaining loyalty he held for the king.

Shortly after this expedition, Adams left to attend the Second Continental Congress scheduled to begin May 10. He returned to Philadelphia with a set goal in mind: convince Congress to create a national army to replace the rough-and-tumble, undisciplined militiamen who had the British troops under siege in Boston. This was no easy task. Congress was so divided that while one committee drafted a petition of reconciliation to the king, another contemplated how to raise money for gunpowder.

Three weeks passed and still no steps had been taken to assist the small New England army surrounding Boston. Then on June 2, an express rider from Boston brought a desperate plea for assistance. Within two weeks the delegates voted to create a Continental army.

The next step was to choose a commander. Massachusetts delegate, John Hancock, coveted the post, but Adams favored George Washington, who was better known because of his role in the French and Indian War. Also, as a southerner he could unite the North and South in their common cause. Equally important to Adams was his conviction that Washington would not abuse the power entrusted to him.

On June 14, 1775, Adams nominated Washington to command the new army. He was delighted when the

The Declaration of Independence was signed at the Philadelphia State House, which was later renamed Independence Hall.

delegates unanimously elected the stately Virginian. Nonetheless, watching Washington and his officers ride out of Philadelphia with bands playing and people cheering, Adams felt a twinge of envy. "Such is the Pride and Pomp of War," he wrote in his dairy. "I, poor Creature, worn out with scribbling, for my Bread and my Liberty . . . must leave others to wear Laurells [honors] which I have Sown; others, to eat the Bread which I have earned . . ."

The decision to raise an army had come none too soon. While Washington was still on his way to Cambridge, a fierce battle was being fought outside Boston for control of Bunker (or Breed's) Hill. Abigail wrote John that she and eight-year-old Johnny had climbed to the top of a hill behind the farm and watched the burning of Charlestown. "My bursting Heart must find vent at my pen," the letter continued. "I have just heard that our dear Friend Dr. [Joseph] Warren is no more but fell gloriously fighting for his Country . . . Great is our loss."

Adams praised Abigail for her bravery. "It gives me more Pleasure than I can express . . . that you sustain with so much Fortitude, the Shocks and Terrors of the Times," he wrote her. "You are really brave, my dear, you are an Heroine."

At the end of July the Continental Congress adjourned until September. Adams had planned to surprise his family by arriving at the farm unannounced, but when he heard that the Massachusetts Assembly was meeting in nearby Watertown, he rode directly there instead. While in Watertown, he learned that his brother Elihu, a member of the Massachusetts militia, had died from dysentery. However, Adams had little time to indulge in grief. Even his time with Abigail was limited to weekends at the farm, except for one three-day period when she joined him in Watertown.

September found him back in Philadelphia for the reconvening of Congress. He did not know it, but the dysentery that killed his brother had become an epidemic in Braintree. Abigail and three-year-old Tommy both became deathly ill. Abigail's mother nursed them back to health, but then contracted the disease herself. She died on October 1.

Abigail poured out her grief to John. "I almost am ready to faint under this severe and heavy Stroke, seperated from *thee* who used to be a comfortar towards me in affliction . . ." John's first impulse was to return home. "At this Distance," he agonized, "I can do no good to you nor yours." Nevertheless, he did not leave Philadelphia. And in his next letter, he wrote that he did not know when he would be home. "We have so much to do, and it is so difficult to do it right . . ."

In the meantime, many Americans had begun to speak openly of independence. In Philadelphia, the congressional delegates worked long hours struggling to establish a government capable of waging war. In early December 1775, "worn down with long and uninterrupted Labour," Adams requested leave from Congress and set out for Braintree.

Chapter Six

"We Are in the Very Midst of a Revolution"

After spending only four days at the farm, Adams rode to Watertown and took his seat in the Massachusetts Provincial Congress then in session. He served on eight committees, briefed members on the situation in Philadelphia, and cajoled those who still held out against independence. He devoted the remaining week of his leave to Abigail and the children, then left for Cambridge to confer with Washington. On January 24, 1776, Adams dined with the General and Mrs. Washington, and then set off on horseback to rejoin the Continental Congress.

The march toward independence was gaining momentum. Just two weeks earlier, a writer named Thomas Paine—new to America and living in Philadelphia—had published a pamphlet called *Common Sense*. The radical document urged Americans to declare independence. It sold 120,000 copies and set off a chain reaction of events. In March, Washington and the Continental Army drove the British out of Boston. Congress sent Connecticut delegate Silas Deane to France to request financial and military assistance. By April, the colonies referred to themselves as the United Colonies. Early in May, Adams introduced a resolution that each colony prepare for independence by adopting a new government. Then on June 7, Virginia delegate Richard Henry Lee, made a formal motion calling for independence. When a bitter debate erupted, further discussion was postponed until July 1.

Nevertheless, Adams confidently wrote to a fellow lawyer in Massachusetts: "We are in the very midst of a revolution . . . The Congress must declare the colonies free and independent States . . ."

In the meantime, fighting between British and American soldiers continued. And on June 12, Congress created a Board of War and appointed Adams its president. Taking on this task substantially increased Adams's already staggering workload. His workdays now began at four in the morning and continued until ten at night.

On July 1, Congress again took up the resolution for independence. Outside, a thunderstorm raged, and the room became so dark that the clerk was asked to light candles. John Dickinson, a Pennsylvania delegate, spoke first, passionately protesting separation from the mother country. It was a deeply moving speech. When it ended, the men sat in silence. No one appeared willing to speak.

Then John Adams rose from his chair. Raising his voice to be heard over the crashing thunder, he spoke with fire and determination about the need for independence. It was the most important speech he ever made. Thomas Jefferson said later that Adams spoke "with a power of thought and expression that moved us from our seats." The next day twelve colonies voted for independence. On July 4, the delegates approved the wording of the Declaration of Independence, and an exultant Adams wrote Abigail that "the greatest question . . . which ever was debated in America" had now been decided.

But as president of the Board of War, Adams had little to celebrate. Reports from the front brought only bad news. Washington had moved his troops to New York, hoping to keep New York City out of the hands of the British. But his 20,000 men—faced with a well-equipped professional British army of 32,000—met only defeat. By September, New York was in the hands of the British, and Washington's army had retreated to New Jersey.

Adams had hoped to spend September with his family. Now he informed Abigail: "Our Affairs having taken a Turn . . . so much to our Disadvantage, I cannot see my Way clear, to return home so soon as I intended." But within a few weeks he changed his mind, writing playfully: "I suppose your Ladyship has been in the Twitters . . . because you have not received a Letter by every Post, as you used to do. But I am coming to make my Apology in Person."

On this trip, Adams devoted much of his time to Abigail. He promised he would never again be away for

General George Washington led the Continental Army against the British.

such an extended period. Massachusetts re-elected him to the Continental Congress during his leave, and after a happy nine weeks at home, Adams returned to Philadelphia. This leave-taking was particularly difficult because Abigail was pregnant—her first pregnancy in six years—and she yearned for John to stay with her.

For his part, Adams wanted to be with his family but he appeared unable to leave the excitement of the political arena. Moreover, he was needed in Congress because others were unwilling to make the sacrifice of long separations from their families. How much of his service was due to a patriotic sense of duty, and how much to his desire for a place in history is impossible to determine. But it was not for money. Adams's legal colleagues in Massachusetts were making a fortune, and he could have been doing the same.

In any case, shortly after New Year's Day 1777, Adams set off on the now familiar journey to Philadelphia. Along the way, he learned of Washington's successful surprise attack on British and Hessian soldiers at Trenton, New Jersey. This crucial victory bolstered the American army's sagging morale, but it was not enough. To defeat a powerful force like England, the new nation needed help. And in January, Congress sent delegates Benjamin Franklin and Arthur Lee to join Silas Deane in his quest for French military support.

Adams continued with his often frustrating duties on the Board of War. He soon learned that not all colonists

Benjamin Franklin traveled to France to request aid during the American Revolution.

were as avid as he in their support of independence. He was appalled by the reluctance of many to bear arms or to serve in Congress.

Meanwhile, in Braintree, Abigail struggled with what she called her "situation." She had no hope of John being home for the baby's birth, and this time she would not have her mother's comfort and support. When a neighbor died in childbirth, Abigail's uneasiness increased. "I have many anxieties, some of which . . . [would be] greatly alleviated if you could be with me," she wrote John.

Adams appeared strangely insensitive to her fears. Many of his return letters dealt only with his own physical complaints or with questions about the farm. On July 10, however, as the baby's birth neared, he wrote tenderly: "My Mind is again Anxious, and my Heart in Pain for my dearest Friend . . . Oh that I could be near, to say a few kind Words . . . or do a few kind Actions . . . Oh that I could take from my dearest, a share of her Distress."

Three days later Adams learned that the baby had been born dead. It was a cruel blow, made more difficult for Abigail because the baby was a girl. "My Heart was much set upon a Daughter," she wrote. But John, too, was shaken. "Is it not unaccountable," he wrote her, "that one should feel so strong an Affection for an Infant, that one has never seen, nor shall see? Yet I must confess to you, the Loss of this sweet little Girl, has most tenderly and sensibly affected me."

The war did not pause for personal sorrow. By September 1777, the British occupied Philadelphia. Adams and the other Congressmen had fled to York, Pennsylvania. The war was not going well for America. In his diary, Adams wrote: "The Prospect is chilling, on every Side. Gloomy, dark, melancholly, and dispiriting." But then in mid-October, the Continental Army scored a major victory at Saratoga, New York—a triumph that would ultimately convince France to enter the war as America's ally.

Now Adams felt free to leave Congress and go home to stay. He told Abigail that he would refuse reelection to Congress and resume his law practice. But in November, Silas Deane—suspected of unethical behavior—was recalled from France, and Congress appointed Adams to replace him. Adams, apparently, never considered refusing the commission. He wrote to Benjamin Rush on February 8, 1778: "Whether I shall be able to render any valuable service to our country in my new capacity . . . is to me very uncertain. All I can say with confidence is, that . . . I will never knowingly do it any injury."

Abigail was heartbroken. At first she insisted that she and the children go with him. But that was impractical; Congress would not pay for their passage or for their living expenses in Paris. In the end it was decided that John Quincy—now ten years old—would benefit from foreign travel, and thus should accompany his father. The two sailed on the *Boston* on February 13, 1778.

Adams's stay in France was difficult. France had

already agreed to help America, so there was little work to be done. With his usual honesty, Adams wrote Congress that there was no need for three commissioners in France. One, he said, would be adequate. He wrote this knowing that if Congress heeded his advice, he would be recalled and the popular Franklin would be chosen to remain. While he waited for a response, Adams devoted his time to sorting out the masses of paperwork that Deane had left in shambles.

At last he received word that Franklin would now be the sole commissioner in Paris. Congress did not actually recall Adams to America, but he decided to return anyway. He and John Quincy reached Braintree in August 1779, having been away for a year and a half. Pleased to be back Adams stayed close to home, spending precious time with Abigail and becoming reacquainted with his other children.

But within two months, he learned that Congress had designated him to negotiate a peace treaty with Great Britain. Congressional delegates believed that the war would soon end, and when it did they wanted an American peace negotiator on hand in Europe. For Adams the assignment meant returning to France.

He accepted the commission immediately. On this trip he took with him, not only John Quincy, but nine-year-old Charles as well. Left behind were Nabby, now fourteen, seven-year-old Thomas, and of course, Abigail. By February 1780, Adams had re-settled in Paris and enrolled both boys in boarding school. He had little to do but wait, not a pleasant prospect for such an energetic man. As a result, he made a nuisance of himself by repeatedly urging the French minister to increase France's military presence in America. Franklin, who felt it was unwise to push France too hard, complained to Congress: "Mr. Adams has given offense to the [French] court."

Recognizing that his usefulness in France was limited, Adams turned his attention to Holland. He had two objectives: persuade the Dutch to acknowledge America as an independent nation, and procure a loan so that America would not be totally dependent on France. As he often did, Adams was taking things into his own hands. He had no official status in Holland. Only later did he learn that Congress had already commissioned him minister to that country.

Adams took his two sons with him to Holland, placing them first in the Latin School at Amsterdam, and then transferring them to the University of Leyden. But that arrangement ended in July 1781 when Adams's secretary, Francis Dana, was appointed minister to Russia. Dana spoke neither Russian nor French, and he asked if John Quincy—now fourteen and proficient in French—could travel with him as his interpreter. Adams granted permission.

Shortly after John Quincy's departure, Charles fell seriously ill. He recovered, but he was unhappy without his brother. And he missed his mother and his friends in

Braintree. Adams, concerned about the boy's health, wrote Abigail that he was sending Charles home.

At the end of 1781, Adams received the welcome news that the Americans had defeated the British at Yorktown, Virginia. Winning this battle ensured that America would win the war. And the Dutch, who had refused to recognize either America's independence or Adams's diplomatic status, now experienced a swift change of heart. Consequently, Adams negotiated a treaty of goodwill and secured the first of four loans—a total of $3.5 million— which the fledgling American government desperately needed. This was a personal victory for Adams who had faced ridicule from both Franklin and the French minister when he first began courting the Dutch.

By this time, Congress had decided to entrust English peace negotiations to a commission which included Benjamin Franklin and John Jay—rather than to Adams alone. In October, 1782, Adams left Holland to join Franklin and Jay in Paris where the peace talks were already underway. Discussion and negotiations continued into 1783. Finally, in September, the peace treaty was signed, formally ending the eight-year war with England.

But still Adams could not return home. Congress asked him to remain in France and help arrange commercial treaties with various European countries. Weary and lonely, he wrote Abigail: "I must stay another Winter. I cannot justify going home. But what shall I do for Want of my Family . . . Will you come to me this fall . . .?"

By the time Abigail received John's letter, winter had set in, making ocean travel too dangerous. Instead she made plans to sail in the spring. She would take Nabby with her, and leave the two younger children, Charles and Thomas, with relatives. It pained Abigail to leave her home, her country and her children. And she dreaded the long ocean voyage. "I console myself," she wrote John, "with the Idea of being joyfully and tenderly received by the best of Husbands and Friends . . ." With the exception of three short months, the two had been apart for six years.

Chapter Seven

Ambassador Adams in the Motherland

After a four-week voyage, Abigail and Nabby arrived in England on July 21, 1784. They traveled by carriage to London—a three-day-journey—and took rooms in a hotel in Covent Gardens. American friends informed Abigail that John was in Holland, and she wrote to him there. Twenty days passed before she received an answer. These were days of anxiety for Abigail, who feared their first meeting would be awkward after being apart for so long.

At last she received John's reply. "Your letter has made me the happiest man upon Earth," he wrote. "I am twenty Years younger than I was Yesterday." The couple's reunion apparently went well, and by August the family had settled into a lovely country house in Auteuil, a suburb of Paris. It was an especially golden time because Abigail had not seen John Quincy for five years, and it had been the same amount of time since John had seen Nabby.

Adams's happiness was enhanced by Thomas Jefferson's arrival in Paris. The two men were opposite in temperament, but they got along well; as did Jefferson and Abigail. But the Adamses stay in France was destined to be brief.

In the spring of 1785, Adams was appointed America's first ambassador to England. His selection caused controversy in Congress, and Adams was hurt when he learned of the deep hostility some delegates displayed toward him. Nonetheless, he had coveted the English ambassadorship, and he had never felt at home in France. He would, however, be sorry to say goodbye to Jefferson, who had now replaced Franklin as minister to France. Abigail wrote Jefferson that she was "[reluctant] . . . to leave behind . . . the only person with whom [John] could associate with perfect freedom and unreserve."

Before John and Abigail left for England, they had to decide what to do with John Quincy, now almost eighteen. Abigail did not want to be separated from her oldest son again, but both parents eventually agreed that he should complete his education in America. Consequently, John Quincy returned to Massachusetts and entered the junior class at Harvard University.

To be an American ambassador to Great Britain in 1785 was a difficult task. Americans were no longer part of the British Empire, and a bitter England was not about to help her former colonists. The trade outlets that had been available to American colonies were no longer open to independent American states. Adams's first objective was to persuade England to reopen its ports to American ships. Secondly, he hoped to induce the government to withdraw its remaining garrisons from the American northwest as stipulated in the peace treaty. Adams soon learned that any chance of achieving these goals was remote.

In the meantime, John and Abigail, along with Nabby, moved into a large townhouse in one corner of London's Grosvenor Square. The Adams house became the headquarters for American businessmen, students, and other travelers in London. Unhappy homesick Loyalists, who had been exiled or had left America voluntarily during the Revolution, came to Adams seeking aid.

Few Americans were popular in England at this point. But Adams was particularly disliked because the British knew he had been instrumental in America's decision to declare independence. Whatever he tried to do was met with polite, cold indifference. His discussions with Lord Carmarthen, England's foreign secretary, led nowhere. "No step that I can take, no language I can hold, will do any good, or, indeed, much harm."

In December 1785, Adams submitted a letter to Carmarthen repeating his request that England uphold the peace treaty and remove British outposts from the American northwest. The secretary took three months to respond. When he did, he said in effect that the Americans were not living up to their part of the treaty so why should the British. Unfortunately, there was truth in this. American debts to English creditors had not been paid because Congress had neither the power nor the money to pay them. With no bargaining leverage, Adams could do little.

Despite Adams's diplomatic frustrations, this was a happy time for him personally. He did not have his three sons with him, but he did have Abigail and Nabby. His contentment was reflected in his health, which was better than it had been for a long time. A continuing exchange of letters with Jefferson also afforded him pleasure.

Abigail, however, was not as content. She disliked England, and she was homesick for her sons. One comfort was that her daughter's life appeared settled. Before leaving Massachusetts, Nabby had been in love with a young man named Royall Tyler. She expected to return and marry him, but the relationship could not weather their separation. Soon fewer and fewer letters arrived from Tyler, and in late summer of 1785, Nabby broke off the engagement. By early 1786, she was engaged to Colonel William Smith, a thirty-year-old bachelor who had been assigned by Congress to act as Adams's secretary. They were married in June, and both John and Abigail approved of the union.

That same year, Adams began writing an essay that grew into a three-volume work called *A Defence of the Constitutions of Government of the United States of America*. In it he maintained that balanced power was the first principle of good government, and that the passions of the people must be restrained for the common good. The first volume was published early in 1787, just as reports from home were making it increasingly clear that government under the Articles of Confederation was not working. Americans—weary of high taxes and tired of petitioning a legislature that lacked power to help them— had begun taking the law into their own hands.

Adams's ambassadorship in England would expire in another year, and in January he wrote Congress requesting that his appointment not be extended. He was frustrated with the ongoing resistance of the English government to negotiation, and both he and Abigail longed to see their sons. "To be explicit," Adams wrote, "I am determined to come home."

But by May 1787, fifty-five delegates had gathered in Philadelphia to create a new Constitution for the thirteen American states. As a result, no immediate action was taken on Adams's request to return home. Nevertheless, he began winding up his affairs in Europe and arranging for his return voyage. Finally in December he received notice from Congress that "the [honorable] John Adams . . . be permitted agreeably to . . . return to America . . ."

At Jefferson's urging however, Adams made one last trip to Holland. Interest was coming due on money borrowed from France during the Revolution, and Congress had no money to pay it. Although Adams had no authorization to do so, he secured a fourth loan from the

A

D E F E N C E

OF THE

CONSTITUTIONS of GOVERNMENT

OF THE

UNITED STATES of AMERICA.

By JOHN ADAMS, LL.D.

AND A MEMBER OF THE ACADEMY OF ARTS AND SCIENCES
AT BOSTON.

All nature's difference keeps all nature's peace.   Pope.

L O N D O N:

PRINTED FOR C. DILLY, IN THE POULTRY

M.DCC.LXXXVII.

John Adams published many political writings throughout his career.

Dutch which saved America, as well as Jefferson, from embarrassment.

John and Abigail departed England on April 20, 1788, and reached Boston in June—one day after the new Constitution was ratified. John Hancock, now governor of Massachusetts, had arranged an elaborate reception. A large crowd of people greeted them at the Boston pier. They were escorted to the governor's mansion in the official carriage. Along the way people lined the roadsides, and each town fired a cannon salute and rang its church bells. It was a welcome that far surpassed any of Adams's early dreams of fame and recognition.

Adams was returning to a very different America. Much had occurred in the nine years he had been away. Politically, he was out of touch. He did not know whether he should think in terms of holding a federal or a state office. But there was no need for an immediate decision. He would first seek the much-needed serenity of Braintree and the companionship of the sons he had been separated from for so long. Personal business that had been long neglected must also be seen to, and the larger house he had purchased while in London needed renovating. Only then would he test the political winds and take stock of the future. He could not have projected that in less than a year he would hold the second highest post in the new national government.

Chapter Eight

Honor and Censure

John and Abigail were excited to be reunited with their three sons—the first time in nine years that all three boys had been together with their parents. Charles and Thomas were now students at Harvard, and John Quincy, who had graduated the previous summer, was clerking in a Boston law office. Only Nabby, living in New York, was missing from the family circle.

Adams, as he had often done in the past, insisted that he had no further interest in politics. He unpacked the large number of books he had purchased abroad, enjoyed long meandering walks around his farm, visited old friends like Richard Cranch, and spent time with his mother—now nearly eighty. In January 1789, he wrote Jefferson: "I have enjoyed a Luxury for the last Six Months which I have [not] tasted for, at least eight and twenty Years . . ."

Adams could not stay idle for long, however. Soon a president and vice-president would be elected to lead the nation under the new Constitution. The only man being considered for president was George Washington, a Virginian. The second position would probably go to a New Englander.

Candidates were not elected by popular vote. Instead, electors—chosen by each state—cast two ballots without designating which one was for the presidency and which one was for the vice-presidency. The man receiving the largest number of electoral votes became president, while the one receiving the second largest became vice-president.

When the electors voted in March 1789, Washington was elected unanimously. Adams, who received the next highest number of votes, became vice-president. Abigail was pleased because New York City was now the home of the national government, and John's election meant they could live near Nabby and the grandchildren. She would remain in Braintree for the time being, however, because no salary had yet been provided for the vice-president.

Adams left for New York on April 13 with a military escort. Much to his delight, Boston gave him a grand send-off. He reached New York City a few days before Washington, and was immediately sworn in as vice-president. Washington was inaugurated on April 30, 1789. Unlike future inaugurations, this one not only installed a president, it also instituted a new government. No one knew exactly what to do or how to do it. Every action would create a pattern for the future.

When Adams became vice-president, he was fifty-four years old, bald, and portly. A slight tremor of his hands, which had begun years ago, was becoming increasingly noticeable. Like everyone else, he was uncertain how to proceed. The vice-president's duties were not clearly defined beyond the provision that he preside over the Senate, voting only when it was necessary to break a tie. Adams soon discovered that the vice-presidency was not the job he had imagined. He wrote Abigail: "My country has in its wisdom, contrived for me the most insignificant office that ever the invention of man contrived or his imagination conceived."

He had difficulty accepting that he was merely to officiate and leave debating to the senators. He could not keep still. He lectured, expounded, and much to the annoyance of the senators, often reminded them of his superior knowledge of parliamentary procedures and etiquette. His short, fat figure and his lectures on proper etiquette soon earned Adams the title of "His Rotundity."

Adams longed for Abigail, but he could not afford to bring her to New York. Finally, though, he could no longer bear the separation. He wrote her to either borrow the money or "sell Horses oxen Sheeps Cowes, any Thing at any [price] rather than not come . . ." He rented a house for them at Richmond Hill on Staten Island, and Abigail arrived in mid-June.

Two controversial issues faced the second session of Congress in January 1790. One was the Assumption Bill introduced by Secretary of the Treasury, Alexander Hamilton, which provided that the federal government assume the war debts of the various states. Many, including Adams, believed this bill was necessary in order to instill confidence in the government's credit both at home and abroad. Thomas Jefferson, the new Secretary of State, opposed the bill.

The second issue concerned choosing a permanent site for the Federal Government. Thomas Jefferson wanted the capital located in the south. Northerners, naturally, wanted it in the north.

In order to resolve these two thorny issues, Hamilton and Jefferson struck a deal. Hamilton agreed to support a southern site for the national capital if Jefferson backed the Assumption Bill. Both men carried out their pledges. Hamilton got his bill passed, and the south got the capital. Adams was pleased, but Abigail wept when she learned the government would subsequently move to Philadelphia. She did not want to leave Nabby and the grandchildren. "I feel low-spirited and heartless," she wrote her sister Mary.

By December, when the Senate—with Adams presiding—opened its session in Philadelphia's Congress Hall, the French Revolution had begun. The revolt would create the first schism in the Adams-Jefferson friendship. Jefferson, like most Americans, enthusiastically supported the French Revolution. Adams did not. He saw it as a breakdown of law and order that would lead to social anarchy.

Secretary of Treasury Alexander Hamilton supported a strong federal government.

Going against popular opinion, Adams wrote a series of essays on government, which he titled "Discourses on Davila." In them, he appeared to urge the establishment of an aristocratic branch of government in America. When the essays were published, Adams was accused of being a monarchist and an aristocrat, and of hating the plain people. He protested that he had been misunderstood, but trying to explain only made the situation worse. Accusations that he favored rule by a king would follow him for years. In old age, he wrote that the "Davila" essays had "powerfully operated to destroy his popularity."

Adams brooded over the public's lack of appreciation for his services. He knew that he would never attain the revered popularity that Franklin and Washington enjoyed. He revealed his bitterness in a letter to Benjamin Rush, writing with withering sarcasm: "The history of our Revolution will be one continued lie from one end to the other. The essence . . . will be *that Dr. Franklin's electrical rod smote the earth and out sprung General Washington . . . and henceforward these two conducted all the policy, negotiation, legislation and war.*"

In March 1791, Thomas Paine's *Rights of Man*—which championed the cause of the French Revolution—was published in England. A copy of it came to Jefferson with instructions to forward it to an American printer. He did so, including a note that he was delighted to see "something was . . . to be publicly said against the political heresies which [have] sprung up among us . . . ." This was

Thomas Jefferson found fault with Adams's "Discourses on Davila" essays.

an obvious reference to Adams's Davila essays. The printer used these comments as a forward to the book. That had not been Jefferson's intent, and he immediately sent an apology to Adams. But the damage had been done.

The second presidential election would take place in November 1792. No one doubted that Washington would be re-elected. However, who would be vice-president was far from certain. By this time two distinct political parties were emerging: the Federalists, who supported a strong national government; and the Republicans, who favored strong states rights and a weak national government.

Adams's major opponent for vice-president was Governor George Clinton of New York. The charge that Adams favored a monarchy soon re-surfaced. The *New York Journal* listed the vice presidential candidates, and warned voters to beware those "who have endeavored to prepare . . . the people of America for a King . . ." Critics also accused Adams of preparing for his own rise to the presidency.

Amidst this turmoil, Adams retreated to Braintree (now called Quincy). He let it be known that he planned to stay there until he knew the outcome of the election. Despite reports that Clinton's strength was growing, Adams refused to budge. One reason was Abigail, whose health remained poor; another was that he did not want to be seen as campaigning for re-election. The election results were released in March 1793. Again Washington won unanimously, and Adams received seventy-seven votes to Clinton's fifty.

Three months after the election, France declared war on both Spain and England. This was bad news because America's treaty with France obligated it to help defend the French West Indies. President Washington, knowing that war must be avoided until America was stronger, proclaimed a policy of strict neutrality. But this was easier said than done.

In 1794, England seized 300 American merchant ships and impressed [forced] hundreds of seamen into service on English vessels. Outraged Americans immediately called for a declaration of war. Instead, Washington sent John Jay, now the Attorney General, to London to negotiate a commercial treaty.

Jay had little to bargain with, and as a result he was forced to make major concessions. England agreed to reimburse American shippers for their losses, but would not pledge to stop capturing American seamen. Americans berated Jay for accepting such terms, but President Washington ignored the public outcry, and used his influence to get Senate approval of the treaty. Adams presided over the Senate deliberations, but of course he could take no part in the debate. The treaty was approved by one vote.

It frustrated Adams that he had little or nothing to do with the great events transpiring around him. He wrote Abigail: "I am wearied to death . . . confined to my seat, as in a prison, to see nothing done, hear nothing said, and to say and do nothing."

Meanwhile, on the domestic front, the Adams children generated both pride and concern. On the plus side, John Quincy had been confirmed by the Senate as ambassador to the Netherlands—the same post Adams himself once held. And Charles and Thomas had passed their bar exams and opened law offices. But Charles was a worry. He had exhibited signs of excessive drinking while at Harvard, and the problem had continued to grow. A further concern was an increasing awareness that Col. William Smith, Nabby's husband, was not the catch that the Adamses first thought. He displayed no business sense, spent money recklessly, and gradually sank deeper and deeper into debt. Nabby and the children were left alone for long periods with little financial support.

As for Adams, he learned in early 1797 that Washington would not accept a third term as president. He wrote Abigail: "I am heir apparent, you know, and a succession is soon to take place." And in another letter: "Either we must enter upon ardors more trying than ever yet experienced; or retire to Quincy, farmers for life." Few, including Abigail, doubted what he would do.

Chapter Nine

President John Adams

The 1796 presidential contest soon narrowed down to Adams and Jefferson. Neither campaigned for election, but their supporters did. The Republicans—Jefferson's party—repeatedly warned that as president Adams would favor England, which would result in America going to war with France. But the Federalists—who supported Adams—countered that Jefferson would form an alliance with France that would lead to war with England.

On February 8, 1797, the electoral ballots were counted. As the vice-president, Adams announced the results to the Senate: Adams seventy-one votes, Jefferson sixty-eight. By receiving the second highest number of votes, Jefferson became Adams's vice-president. Adams had earlier stated that it would create a "dangerous crisis in publick affairs if the President and Vice President should be in opposite boxes [parties]." But Jefferson let it be known immediately that he was delighted to serve under Adams.

John Adams was inaugurated at Congress Hall in

Philadelphia on March 4, 1797, without any of his family present. The next day he wrote Abigail: "A solemn scene it was indeed, and it was made more affecting to me by the presence of the General [Washington] . . . Methought I heard him say, 'Ay! I am fairly out and you fairly in! See which of us will be the happiest.'"

Adams inherited numerous problems from Washington's administration, not the least of which was the former president's cabinet. In particular, Timothy Pickering, the secretary of state; and James McHenry, the secretary of war, were mediocre administrators who rendered no loyalty to Adams. Instead, they took their orders from Alexander Hamilton, the leader of New York's Federalist party, who saw himself as the power behind the throne. Adams was apparently unaware of the connivance taking place behind his back.

In any event, it was the ongoing problems with France and England that presented his immediate challenge. The French, angered by Jay's treaty with England, perceived America as pro-British. Only ten days after Adams took office, the French government ordered Charles C. Pinckney—the American ambassador sent earlier by Washington—to leave France. A few weeks later they ordered neutral vessels transporting British goods seized. Since "neutral vessels" included American ships, immediate action was required by the president.

Above all, Adams wanted to avoid war. Stalling for time, he summoned a special session of Congress to begin in sixty days. His cabinet—urged on by Hamilton—advised war and recommended creating a navy and a standing army. But Adams waited for the special Congress before taking any action.

Abigail had intended to wait until fall to join her husband, but now he pleaded with her to come sooner. "I must go to you or you must come to me," he wrote. "I cannot live without you till October." As soon as the weather warmed, Abigail left for Philadelphia. She stopped in New York to see Nabby, and found her alone with the children, her husband hiding out somewhere to avoid his creditors. It was a distressing visit, and Abigail left with an aching heart.

She arrived in Philadelphia five days before the special Congress convened. Her presence comforted Adams, who was preparing to face grumpy congressmen, unhappy at being recalled to the capital during the sweltering summer months.

When Adams spoke to the Congress on May 15, he expressed outrage at France's treatment of America's ambassador. He made it clear that he would not tolerate any further humiliation of the United States, but he also insisted on "a fresh attempt at negotiation." He proposed to send John Marshall, a Federalist from Virginia, and Elbridge Gerry, a Republican from Massachusetts to join Pinckney, who was still in Europe. The three-man commission was to seek a treaty of commerce and friendship.

The special Congress adjourned on July 10, 1797, and

the Adamses prepared to leave for Quincy. But before departing the capital, Adams—after consulting with Washington—appointed John Quincy ambassador to Russia. Washington expressed warm approval of the appointment, but the Republicans and the press criticized Adams, pointing out that "George Washington had never appointed to any station in government, even the most distant of his relations."

Attacks from the press increased when John Quincy married Louisa Catherine Johnson, the daughter of an affluent Maryland merchant who had lived in England since the end of the war. To many Americans, and especially to the Republicans, Louisa was an English-woman. Even Adams himself said, "I wished in my heart it might have been in America."

When the First Family returned to Philadelphia in November, the president hoped that word from his peace emissaries in France would be waiting. But the only message was that Gerry and Marshall had arrived safely. On November 23, Adams spoke to Congress. He did not go so far as to predict war, but he urged improvement of the country's military defenses, telling the legislators that America must be prepared. He then sought the opinion of Secretary of War James McHenry, who immediately contacted Hamilton. Harboring dreams of military glory, Hamilton proposed that an army of twenty thousand men be raised immediately—a suggestion that McHenry passed on to the president as his own idea.

John Quincy Adams followed his father into politics and in 1825 became the sixth president of the United States.

Meanwhile in France, the peace commissioners were visited by three agents of the French government. These agents suggested that an agreement could be reached in return for a loan from the United States and payment of a $240,000 bribe. Such bribery was common in European politics, but the Americans found these conditions intolerable, and negotiations broke down.

In March 1798, Adams reported to Congress that the peace mission had failed, and he was recalling the three commissioners. "I will never send another minister to France, without assurances that he will be . . . respected, and honored as the representative of a great, free, powerful and independent nation," he vowed angrily. In April, he released details of the bribery attempt to the public. Americans were outraged, and the pressure on Adams from his own party to declare war increased.

Adams took steps to prepare the country for possible war. He created the Department of the Navy under Benjamin Stoddert and brought Washington out of retirement to command the army. Appointing additional officers, however, posed a problem. Everyone knew that Washington was too old to take active command of the army. Therefore, the officer second in command would in reality be the actual commander.

Adams planned to make this appointment on the basis of seniority. But Hamilton, who wanted the number two spot, appealed to Washington to intervene for him. At Washington's urging, Adams appointed Hamilton. He had little choice. Americans revered Washington, and it would have been unwise for Adams to oppose the former president's wishes.

In June 1798, war hysteria led the mostly Federalist Congress to pass the Naturalization, Alien, and Sedition Acts. The Naturalization Act extended the length of time an emigrant had to live in America before being granted citizenship. Two Alien acts gave the president the power to expel foreigners from the country.

But it was the controversial Sedition Act that upset the Republicans. It made illegal "any libellous attack by writing, printing, publishing or speaking" against the president or other top government officials. The law was aimed at silencing the harsh criticism directed against the Federalist Administration by Republican newspapers. Adams did not introduce the laws, or play any direct role in their passage, but neither did he oppose or veto them. According to his later comments, he felt the laws were necessary for national defense.

Congress adjourned in August, and John and Abigail returned to Quincy. Shortly after arriving, Abigail fell seriously ill with an unknown virus. It was not until mid-October that she showed signs of recovery, and a much-relieved Adams could begin devoting more time to government correspondence.

The situation between America and France remained his biggest worry. He decided he had three possible courses of action: ask Congress to declare war, continue to do nothing and wait for developments, or once again send diplomats to France seeking peace. He had already made up his mind about the first option. He knew he would not declare war.

The second week in November, Adams left for Philadelphia. He went alone because Abigail was still too weak to travel. On arrival, he immediately summoned his cabinet. All five advisors recommended doing nothing, and they opposed sending more peace ambassadors to Paris. Adams accepted their advice and so informed Congress on December 8, 1798.

However, early in 1799, Adams's youngest son Thomas—who had been in Europe performing secretarial duties for his brother John Quincy—returned to America. He went directly to see his father because he carried a crucial message from France's foreign minister—Charles M. de Talleyrand-Périgord. The letter stated that any representative "sent by the Government of the United States to France . . . would be . . . received with the [respect] suitable to the envoy of a free, independent and powerful nation."

Without consulting his cabinet or any members of Congress, and knowing he was jeopardizing his political career, Adams notified the Senate that he was sending another diplomat to France. He nominated William Vans Murray, America's ambassador to Holland and a friend of John Quincy's, to undertake this mission.

Hamilton—who had dreamed of commanding a fifty-thousand-man army against the French—was furious, as were other Federalist extremists (called High Federalists). They turned their venom on the president through newspaper editorials and vicious attacks on his character. But Adams stood firm. "I have . . . made up my mind, and I will neither withdraw nor modify [Murray's] nomination."

When the High Federalists could not move Adams from his position, they pressured him to appoint additional commissioners to assist Murray. The president had to compromise, or the Senate would have refused to approve Murray's nomination. He appointed Oliver Ellsworth and William Davie as co-comissioners and instructed them to make immediate preparations to join Murray, already in France.

As soon as this was done, Adams entrusted the details to his cabinet and went home to Quincy. Still unaware of the treachery of his cabinet, Adams wrote a friend that he could run the business of the government from Quincy "as readily as I could do at Philadelphia." Naively, he thought that nothing would be done without his approval. But unknown to Adams, Secretary of State Pickering deliberately delayed the departure of the peace envoys, Davie and Ellsworth. Unfortunately, when a friend wrote to Adams hinting at the deception of his cabinet, Abigail intercepted the letter in a misguided attempt to spare her husband pain.

In August, news of an uprising in France that might

restore its king to the throne, reached Quincy. But despite this new political chaos, dispatches from Murray continued to stress that France still wanted peace with the United States. And Talleyrand sent a second message reassuring Adams that American diplomats would be properly received. Consequently, Adams directed Pickering to ready diplomatic instructions for Davie and Ellsworth so they could leave immediately.

Pickering, still following Hamilton's directions, stalled—taking more than a month for a task that should have required only a day or two. Then he informed Adams that the cabinet members advised against the immediate departure of Davie and Ellsworth. Against his better judgment, Adams accepted Pickering's counsel.

Adams had now been away from the seat of government for six months. He used Abigail's health as an excuse although she had continued to improve. But in late August, Adams received a letter from Benjamin Stoddert, his Navy secretary. Stoddert warned him that "artful, designing men" sought to destroy his peace mission. Adams then made plans to leave for Trenton, where the government had moved temporarily to avoid a Yellow Fever epidemic in Philadelphia.

He did not hurry, but stopped in New York to see his son Charles, now hopelessly in the clutches of alcoholism. Adams showed little compassion for his son's pitiful condition. Instead, he called him "a Madman possessed of the Devil," and vowed never to see him again—a promise he kept. Adams's disappointment in Charles coupled with his concern over Nabby's miserable marriage, moved him to write Abigail: "My children give me more Pain than all my Ennemies."

In Trenton, Adams listened attentively to his cabinet's objections, but he was determined to make one more try for peace. He personally ordered Ellsworth and Davie to leave for France, and they sailed November 3.

When Congress adjourned on May 14, 1800, it marked the last time it would assemble in Philadelphia. It would reconvene in November in Federal City—usually called Washington. Before going to Quincy for the summer, Adams went to inspect the new capital, after which he ordered that all departments of the federal government be ready to assume operations in Washington by June 15.

Adams himself did not return to Washington until mid-October. Abigail followed, stopping in New York as usual. Charles was near death, and Abigail remained at his side for several days before she sadly continued on to the new capital city.

Washington was not truly a city yet, but merely a collection of a few public buildings set along unpaved, muddy streets. John and Abigail would reside in the President's House—later called the White House. None of the rooms were finished entirely, but six were livable. Abigail strung clotheslines across the main conference room and dried her wash there. Adams, on his first night in the house, wrote Abigail: "I pray Heaven to bestow the best of blessings on this house and all that shall hereafter inhabit it. May none but wise and honest men ever rule under this roof."

On November 22, 1800, Adams delivered his annual message to Congress. Only eight days later, Charles Adams's tragic young life ended. He was thirty years old and left behind a wife and two young daughters. His father, unable to forgive him even in death, wrote friends that he mourned "the melancholy death of a once beloved son."

But in Washington, the issue on everyone's mind was the upcoming election. Adams shared the Federalist ticket with Charles C. Pinckney, who had been part of the earlier French peace commission. The Federalist party itself, however, was bitterly divided.

Hamilton revealed his deep hostility to Adams in a published fifty-page letter filled with venomous accusations and a declaration that Adams was "unfit for the office of Chief Magistrate." The Republicans, whose candidates were Thomas Jefferson and New York assemblyman Aaron Burr, used the publication to their political advantage. Adams made no comment on Hamilton's attack except to say, "I am confident, it will do him more harm than me." However, in the end, the allegations would also hurt the president.

The campaign was often a vicious one. The Republicans provided financial aid to several newspapers in exchange for published editorials denouncing the Alien and Sedition Acts passed by Adams and accusing the Federalists of pro-British sentiments. In turn, the Federalists charged that Jefferson was pro-French, and a whisper campaign hinted of his sexual misconduct—a charge neither Abigail nor Adams believed. Nevertheless, the bitter campaign caused a break in the Adams-Jefferson friendship that would not be repaired for many years.

The 1800 presidential election was tight. Adams lost, but in a strange twist, there was no winner. Both Jefferson and Burr each received seventy-three electoral votes (Adams received sixty-five). According to the Constitution, the House of Representatives must choose between candidates in cases of a tie vote. On the thirty-sixth ballot, the tie was broken and Thomas Jefferson became president.

Meanwhile, ten weeks of Adams's presidency remained. It was a difficult time for him. Grief over the loss of his son Charles was now compounded by the rejection of the American people. However, Adams doggedly set about completing the unfinished business of his administration.

Word arrived from France that a peace agreement had been reached. (Had it arrived earlier, Adams might have won re-election.) But Adams was justifiably proud of having placed the welfare of America above his own popularity, and thus keeping the nation out of war at a time when war would have been disastrous for the young republic.

On February 12, 1801, Abigail left for Quincy, and Adams continued his solitary duties. In one of his finest legacies to America, Adams appointed John Marshall Chief Justice of the Supreme Court. Marshall would establish the prestige and independence of the judiciary branch of the government.

Other appointments made during these last weeks were not so impressive. He named his son-in-law surveyor of the Port of New York, a frivolous job that even the inept Colonel Smith could surely handle. And he appointed William Cranch, the son of his old friend Richard, justice of the Circuit Court of Columbia.

On the last night of his presidency, Adams packed his books and papers. Then at 4 A.M. on March 4, 1801, while the city slept, he left the White House bound for Quincy. In another six hours, his once cherished friend, Thomas Jefferson, would take the oath of office. Adams would not be there to see it.

Chapter Ten

"Independence Forever"

John Adams was sixty-two years old when he left public life. He had served his country for more than twenty-five years. During that period, he had often voiced a longing to live the life of a simple farmer. But he found retirement a difficult adjustment after so many years of vigorous activity. At first he did little but agonize over why he had lost the election. Then he briefly considered returning to his long-forsaken law practice. But palsy, combined with an inability to speak clearly (most of his teeth had been extracted), made arguing in court an impossibility. By April, he wrote an old acquaintance: "[Boredom], when it rains on a man in large drops, is worse than one of our north-east storms . . ."

John Quincy soon arrived home from Europe with his wife Louisa and their six-month-old son. They settled in Boston and John Quincy resumed his law practice. Soon, though, he was elected to the state legislature, and in 1803—only seventeen months after his return from Europe—he was elected to the United States Senate.

Adams, meanwhile, attempted off and on to write his autobiography—working on it for brief periods and then putting it aside. He enjoyed letter writing more, and was soon writing regularly to old friends and acquaintances. Benjamin Rush was a favorite correspondent.

In 1808, when James Madison was elected president, he appointed John Quincy ambassador to Russia. John Quincy and Louisa now had three sons. When they sailed for Europe in August 1809, they took their infant son, but left the two older boys with their grandparents. John and Abigail had no need to fear loneliness. Thomas, who had moved in with them four years earlier when he married, still lived there with his wife and baby daughter.

In 1810 Adams turned seventy-five. Many of the political leaders of the Revolutionary years had already died—Thomas Paine, Sam Adams, and John Dickinson among them. But Adams himself—except for the worsening of the palsy and a gradual deterioration of his close vision—maintained remarkably good health. He still enjoyed long horseback rides and walked four miles a day when the weather permitted. Abigail, on the other hand, suffered with numerous illnesses. And the rheumatism that had plagued her for years, had grown so severe that even holding a quill for writing caused unbearable pain.

But in the coming year, John and Abigail endured a series of blows that surpassed any physical pain. In October 1811, Richard Cranch, John's oldest friend and brother-in-law, died after a lengthy illness. The two men had been daily companions since Adams's return to

Quincy, and Richard's death left a painful void. Then two days after Richard's death, his widow Mary died. Abigail was devastated at losing her sister who had been a friend as well. But worse was to come.

In the summer, Nabby was told by her doctors in New York that she had breast cancer. Abigail pleaded with her to come home and consult with Boston's leading physicians. Nabby agreed to come, arriving in July. In October, after receiving conflicting medical advice, she finally decided to undergo a mastectomy. The surgery was performed without anesthesia, and Nabby suffered ghastly, excruciating pain during the procedure. But the surgeons assured her she could expect a full recovery. She remained with John and Abigail until she regained her strength, then returned to New York in the summer of 1812.

On a happier note, Benjamin Rush had been trying for two years to rekindle the old friendship between Adams and Jefferson. He wrote repeatedly to both men urging reconciliation. Finally, Adams wrote Rush: "Why do you make so much ado about nothing? Of what use can it be for Jefferson and me to exchange letters? I have nothing to say to him, but to wish him an easy journey to heaven . . . And he can have nothing to say to me . . ."

Yet only a week later, Adams sent Jefferson a packet of John Quincy's lectures and a note wishing him "many happy New Years." Jefferson responded quickly, writing that "no circumstances have lessened . . . my sincere esteem for you." They had always enjoyed exchanging ideas, and soon letters were once again speeding back and forth between them.

At first, Adams dredged up old political disagreements, but he quickly realized that Jefferson's friendship was more important to him than trying to prove he had been right in the past. He began to avoid controversial subjects and focused on philosophical and theological matters, or reminiscences about the Revolution. "Every line from you," he wrote Jefferson in one letter, "exhilarates my spirits and gives me a glow of pleasure . . ."

His pleasure was overshadowed by news that Nabby's cancer had returned and spread throughout her body. In July 1812, she came home "to close her days under the parental roof." She lived only two weeks after her return. The grief-stricken Adams wrote to Jefferson: "My only daughter expired Yesterday Morning in the Arms of Her Husband, her Son, her Daughter, [and] her Father and Mother." Nabby was forty-nine years old.

In the next three years death claimed other friends and relatives. Abigail was shaken by the death of her youngest and only remaining sister Elizabeth. But there was joy also. Nabby's daughter Caroline, who came to live with them after her mother's death, was married in her grandparents' home. And in 1816, John and Abigail rejoiced when John Quincy returned from Russia.

By this time, Abigail had grown quite frail. And Adams, now eighty-two, could barely write because of what he called his "quivering fingers." His eyes had now grown so weak, he could only read for short periods at

John and Abigail Adams's oldest child, Nabby Smith, died in her parents' home.

a time. Nevertheless, these infirmities could not dim the joy of having his son home again.

Adams had always assumed that because he was older than Abigail he would die first. But in the fall of 1818—less than a week before their fifty-fourth wedding anniversary—Abigail contracted typhoid fever. At first it appeared she would recover, but on October 26 her condition worsened. She died two days later at the age of seventy-four. John was desolate. He had always been the one to leave, now he was the one left behind. "The dear Partner of my Life for fifty four Years as a Wife and for many Years more as a Lover, now lyes in extremis, forbidden to speak or be spoken to," he wrote Jefferson.

Adams, however, was not the kind of man to give in to depression and grief. And fortunately, he was surrounded by an extended family who cared for him. He remained reasonably well for several years after Abigail's death, but by 1823 his physical condition had deteriorated considerably. His eyesight grew so dim that he had to dictate his letters and prevail on the grandchildren to read to him. Mentally, however, he remained as sound and alert as ever.

In 1825, Adams savored a final triumph when John Quincy took office as the sixth president of the United States. He was too frail to attend his son's inauguration, and had to settle for writing a letter. "The multitude of my thoughts, and the intensity of my feelings are too much for a mind like mine, in its ninetieth year," he told his son.

"May the blessing of God Almighty continue to protect you to the end of your life . . ."

Adams grew increasingly feeble, and within a year had to be carried up and down the stairs. "I am certainly very near the end of my life," he informed Jefferson early in the year of 1826. But he had one last goal: to live until the fiftieth anniversary of the signing of the Declaration of Independence.

The town of Quincy was preparing a grand ceremony to commemorate the Declaration, and officials begged him to attend and make one last speech. But his health would not permit it. Finally, in June, a member of the celebration committee visited Adams and asked him to provide a toast which would be presented as coming from him. "I will give you," Adams said, "Independence Forever." Asked if he wanted to add anything else, he answered: "Not a word."

On the morning of July 4, Adams could not rise from his bed, but he was alert and aware of the date. In mid-morning, breathing became difficult and he lapsed into unconsciousness. At noon, he revived for a brief period. An hour later, he whispered his last words: "Thomas Jefferson still survives." But he was wrong. In an eerie coincidence, Jefferson had died just a few hours before Adams spoke those words.

At sunset, John Adams—the son of a Braintree farmer, the "Atlas of American Independence"—drew one last ragged breath and joined his old friend and foe in death.

Timeline

1735—John Adams born in Braintree (later Quincy), MA.

1751—Enters Harvard College.

1755—Graduates from Harvard; becomes Worcester
       schoolmaster.

1756—Begins legal studies with James Putnam.

1758—Admitted to bar; practices in Braintree.

1762—Begins fourteen years of traveling the court circuit.

1764—Marries Abigail Smith.

1765—Opposes Stamp Act.

       —Abigail Adams (Nabby) born.

1767—John Quincy Adams born.

1768—Susanna Adams born.

1770—Susanna Adams dies.

       —Boston Massacre occurs.

       —Charles Adams born.

       —Defends and wins acquittal for British defendants in Boston
          Massacre trials.

       —Elected to Massachusetts House of Representatives.

1772—Thomas Boylston Adams born.

1773—Boston Tea Party.

1774—Elected Massachusetts delegate to the First Continental
       Congress.

1775—Battles of Lexington and Concord.
　—Delegate to Second Continental Congress.
　—Nominates George Washington commander of American
　　forces.
1776—*Common Sense* published.
　—British evacuate Boston.
1778—Replaces Silas Deane as joint commissioner to France.
　—Sails with John Quincy for France.
1779—Returns to America.
　—Drafts Massachusetts Constitution.
　—Elected minister to negotiate peace treaty with Britian.
　—Returns to France with sons John Quincy and Charles.
1782—Signs friendship treaty with the Dutch and secures a loan
　　for the United States government.
1783—Signs peace treaty with Britain to end the Revolutionary
　　War.
1784—Executes second Dutch loan.
　—Abigail and Nabby arrive in London.
1785—Appointed first American ambassador to England.
1787—Publishes first two volumes of *A Defence of the
　　Constitutions of the United States of America.*
　—Constitutional Convention held in Philadelphia.
1788—Publishes third volume of *A Defence of the
　　Constitutions.*
　—Negotiates two additional loans from the Dutch.
　—Returns to America.
1789—Elected vice-president.
1790—Begins publishing "Discourses on Davila."
1793—Re-elected vice-president.
1796—Elected second president of the United States.
1797—Appoints first peace mission to France.
　—XYZ Affair.

1798—Signs Alien and Sedition Acts.

1799—Sends second peace commission to France.

1800—Loses election for a second presidential term.

—Open rift develops between Adams and Thomas Jefferson.

—Charles Adams dies.

1801—Appoints John Marshall Chief Justice of the Supreme Court.

—Retires to Quincy.

1812—Renews friendship with Jefferson.

1813—Nabby Adams Smith dies of cancer.

1818—Abigail Adams dies.

1825—John Quincy Adams elected president of the United States.

1826—John Adams dies at Quincy, July 4.

—Thomas Jefferson dies at Monticello, July 4.

Chapter Notes

CHAPTER ONE

p. 9: According to the calendar used in 1735, John Adams was born October 19. However, the new style calendar adopted after his birth changed the date to October 30.

p. 9: John Adams Sr. served Braintree as a church deacon, a tax collector, a militia officer and a selectman.

p. 10: This was the New England Primer, first published in the late 1600s. Six to eight million copies of this popular little book were sold during the century and a half that it remained in print.

p. 11: The primary emphasis at the Latin School was on Latin. However, rhetoric, logic and arithmetic were also taught along with brief surveys of navigation, geography and astronomy.

p. 13: Adams began keeping a diary while he was a student at Harvard. He continued to do so throughout his life, although long periods passed during which he made no entries.

p. 16: By apprenticing himself to an established lawyer, Adams was following the accepted eighteenth century method of preparing for the bar. No law schools existed in the colonies.

CHAPTER TWO

p. 18: Robert Treat Paine and Samuel Quincy were both aspiring young lawyers. In 1770, they would oppose Adams in the Boston Massacre trials.

p. 20: It was over a tea table at Hannah Quincy's house that John and Hannah had engaged in their first intimate conversation.

p. 22: The Massachusetts Superior Court held court in nearly every county in Massachusetts at least once a year—more often in Boston's county. When the allotted time expired in one place, the court moved to the next scheduled county.

CHAPTER THREE

p. 25: In England, the French and Indian War was known as the Seven Years' War.

p. 25: The Stamp Act required colonists to pay a surcharge on legal documents such as wills, deeds, and insurance polices. Newspapers, almanacs, and pamphlets had to be printed on stamped paper that was taxed.

p. 25: Colonial Americans continued to share the political ideas of England, but important ideological differences had developed. England, for example, considered all people in her empire to be virtually, or indirectly, represented. However, in the colonies, the concept of absolute direct representation had evolved.

p. 29: As a selectman, Adams would oversee public schools and road construction, as well as vote to allocate money for aiding the poor.

p. 29: In his entire political career, Adams never campaigned for an office.

p. 30: Dr. Warren also cared for the medical needs of the Adams children.

p. 30: If the colonists tried to import the items affected by the Townshend Acts from other countries, they would be in violation of the Navigation Acts passed in the seventeenth century. Consequently, they resorted to smuggling.

p. 31: Jonathon Sewell had accepted another appointment as Judge of Admiralty in Halifax which left the position of Chief prosecutor vacant.

p. 32: In August 1765, the Sons of Liberty had ravaged and looted Thomas Hutchinson's house.

CHAPTER FOUR

p. 35: Sam Adams christened the shootings "The Boston Massacre."

p. 36: It was important that Preston and the soldiers be tried separately. Preston had not actually killed anyone. But if he were tried with the soldiers—and the prosecution proved he had ordered them to fire—the jury would have to find him guilty of murder since the soldiers would have had no choice but to obey his orders.

p. 37: The "benefit of clergy" plea originated as a protection for priests. Defendants proved they were men of the cloth by demonstrating they could read. Later the plea came to be used by anyone who could read. The brand on the thumbs marked the person as a convicted felon who could never use the plea again.

p. 39: Bohea tea was a black tea grown in China.

p. 40: Britain passed a Tea Act giving the East India Company a monopoly on tea imported into the colonies. The colonists opposed the monopoly, and they called the tax on the tea taxation without representation.

p. 40: Each colony maintained a group of armed volunteers—called a militia—for emergencies.

p. 40: Adams bought the birthplace house from his brother Peter.

p. 41: One of the five Massachusetts delegates to the First Continental Congress did not attend. The four who did were John and Sam Adams, Robert Treat Paine, and Thomas Cushing.

CHAPTER FIVE
p. 42: Philadelphia, in 1774, was the virtual capital of the colonies.

p. 43: Carpenters' Hall was a private building owned by the Carpenters' Guild [union].

p. 44: Paul Revere, a silversmith by trade, was a radical patriot. He served as a spy, an express rider, and eventually as an officer in the Continental Army.

p. 44: After the British seized gunpowder stored by Massachusetts patriots, a group of outraged delegates from Suffolk County— acting in the role of the suspended Massachusetts assembly—drew up the Suffolk Resolves.

p. 45: The *Boston Gazette* essays were signed "Novanglus," but it was common knowledge that Adams was the author.

p. 46: There were new faces at the second Congress: John Hancock had been added to the Massachusetts delegation, Benjamin Franklin had joined the Pennsylvania delegates, and Thomas Jefferson would soon arrive from Virginia.

p. 48: The British Parliament had suspended the Massachusetts Assembly. Unable to meet in Boston, the assemblymen met illegally in Watertown.

p. 49: Dysentery was an intestinal infection that caused vomiting, fever and diarrhea.

p. 49: In the two years following the opening of the Second Continental Congress, Adams sat on ninety committees, chairing twenty-five.

p. 49: The Congress conceived the Articles of Confederation, a government that gave each individual state considerable power, but little to the Continental Congress. Congress could declare war and raise an army and navy, but it had no way to raise money. Congress could request money but could not compel the states to give it.

CHAPTER SIX
p. 50: By the end of 1775, assemblies—because the British had suspended their right to meet—called themselves provincial congresses.

p. 50: Adams bought two copies of *Common Sense*, one for himself and one to send to Abigail.

p. 50: Many Americans originally thought Adams had written the anonymously published *Common Sense.*

p. 51: Adams's resolution was, in effect, a declaration of independence because its preamble stated clearly that the colonists could no longer support a government under the king.

p. 51: Adams seconded the motion for independence.

p. 52: Before adjourning, the delegates appointed a committee to prepare a formal declaration so that if Congress should agree on independence, the document would be ready. The committee included John Adams, Thomas Jefferson, and Benjamin Franklin.

p. 52: New York abstained in the vote for independence.

p. 52: The Declaration of Independence was not actually signed until August.

p. 54: Hessians were German mercenary soldiers with a reputation for cruelty.

p. 57: Benjamin Rush, a Philadelphia physician and one of the signers of the Declaration of Independence was a friend of both John Adams and Thomas Jefferson.

p. 57: John Quincy lived in a boarding school in a suburb of Paris; he spent weekends with his father.

p. 58: The same month that Adams returned from France, he served as Braintree's representative at a state convention where he wrote the state constitution for Massachusetts

p. 58: On his second trip to France, Adams took Francis Dana, a young Boston lawyer, as his diplomatic secretary and John Thaxter as a private secretary and tutor for the boys.

p. 59: Special permission had to be obtained before Charles, only eleven years old, could be accepted at Leyden.

p. 59: French was a universal language in the nineteenth century.

p. 60: Charles's ocean crossing was a perilous one. For four months, John and Abigail worried that he had been lost at sea. He arrived home five months after his ship left France.

p. 60: Seven thousand British soldiers surrendered at Yorktown.

p. 60: John Jay, who had served in both Continental Congresses, was serving as America's ambassador to Spain when Congress appointed him to the peace commission. Thomas Jefferson and Congressman Henry Laurens were also appointed, but Jefferson could not accept because of his wife's illness, and Laurens, unbeknownst to Congress, had been captured by the British.

p. 60: When Adams learned that John Quincy had returned from Russia and was back in Holland, he left the peace talks long enough to go and bring him to Paris.

p. 60: Terms of the peace treaty favored the United States. England fully recognized American independence and promised to withdraw all troops as soon as possible. New boundary lines favored the former colonists who agreed only to pay all debts owed England, and allow Loyalists who had fled the colonies to return without fear of persecution.

CHAPTER SEVEN
p. 62: Adams did not know on which ship, or on what date, Abigail and Nabby would arrive, so he could not arrange to meet them.

p. 64: Adams deliberately sought out one Loyalist, his old friend Jonathan Sewell, who had moved to England in 1775. The two men enjoyed a happy reunion, but despite Adams's efforts, they never resumed their old relationship.

p. 65: Royall Tyler became a playwright and moved to New York, where he wrote *The Contrast*, America's first successful stage play.

p. 65: William Smith graduated from Princeton in 1774 and studied law briefly. He served in the Continental Army throughout the Revolutionary War.

p. 65: In Massachusetts a group of farmers, led by Daniel Shays (Shays' Rebellion), tried to hold off judgments of debt by preventing county courts from convening.

p. 65: In April 1787, John and Abigail became grandparents when Nabby gave birth to a son.

p. 65: *A Defence of the Constitutions of Government of the United States of America* was an unorganized, hastily written work, but according to Adams it was used as a reference at the Constitutional Convention.

p. 66: The Articles of Confederation served as America's first constitution after independence was declared, but the Articles did little more than authorize Congress to run the war.

p. 66: Adams was not present at the Constitutional Convention, but the new Constitution reflected the Massachusetts Constitution authored by Adams.

p. 68: The "new" house was only a mile away from Adams's birthplace. He named it "Peacefield." Other family members called it "The Old House," because it had been built in the early seventeenth century.

CHAPTER EIGHT
p. 69: Adams's youngest son, Thomas, had not been at his father's side since he was a small boy of seven.

p. 69: A few weeks after John and Abigail departed England, Nabby also left, sailing with her husband and son for New York where they would be living.

p. 69: Books were Adams's passion—his one extravagance—and he purchased them with abandon.

p. 70: In 1789, candidates did not campaign, but stood aloof from the process.

p. 70: Adams would have received more votes, but Washington's long-time aide, Alexander Hamilton, was concerned that Adams might amass too many popular votes and end up president. To prevent this, he manipulated the number of votes for Adams by asking friends in certain states to scatter their votes among other candidates.

p. 70: Abigail had traveled alone to New York the previous November when Nabby gave birth to her second child.

p. 70: The vice-presidential salary, when established, was $4,000 a year.

p. 71: The writers of the Constitution created the office of vice-president to provide a successor if the president died or became too ill to function.

p. 71: During his vice-presidency, Adams cast the tie-breaking vote at least thirty-one times—more than any other vice-president in history.

p. 72: The Compromise of 1790 created Washington, D.C. as the permanent capital of the United States. It also decreed that the national government would immediately move from New York to Philadelphia, remaining there until the permanent capital was completed.

p. 74: Henrico Caterino Davila was an Italian political theorist and historian.

p. 74: Among his other accomplishments, Benjamin Franklin was famous for his studies and experiments with lightning and electricity.

p. 76: The Federalists included Hamilton, Washington, and Adams, although Adams was too independent to be truly affiliated with any one party. The Republicans included Jefferson and James Madison.

p. 76: In 1792, following a dispute over school funds, North Braintree broke away from the town of Braintree and became the independent township of Quincy.

CHAPTER NINE

p. 79: The Republican party now called itself Democratic-Republicans, but it was still commonly referred to as the Republican party.

p. 79: In 1804, the twelfth amendment to the Constitution ensured that the president and vice-president would be from the same party in the future.

p. 80: The peaceful transfer of power from Washington to Adams—so unlike the often bloody power shifts in Europe—was an encouraging sign for the American republic.

p. 80: During Washington's eight years in office, most of his original cabinet members (including Jefferson and Hamilton) resigned their posts to return to private life. Because cabinet members received such low pay, it was difficult for Washington to find equally able men to replace them.

p. 80: In 1796, there was no precedent for each administration to appoint its own cabinet members.

p. 82: Some thought it unwise for the president to be away from the capital city during the French crisis. But Washington had set this precedent by returning to Mount Vernon each year for a few weeks of rest.

p. 84: The peace commissioners had difficulty pronouncing the names of the French agents, and so referred to them as X, Y and Z. Thus this bribery attempt entered history as the "XYZ Affair."

p. 85: Seventeen newspaper men and officeholders were indicted under the Sedition Act. Ten were convicted.

p. 87: Oliver Ellsworth was the chief justice who had administered the oath of office to Adams. William Davie, governor of North Carolina, was appointed after Adams's first choice, Patrick Henry, declined to serve.

p. 88: In May 1800, Adams fired cabinet members Pickering and McHenry, replacing McHenry with an old Massachusetts friend, and appointing John Marshall to succeed Pickering as Secretary of State.

p. 89: The government of the young republic was still so small that only seven packing cases held the records to be transferred from Philadelphia to Washington.

p. 90: Hamilton's bitter publication denouncing Adams was titled "Letter Concerning the Public Conduct and Character of John Adams."

p. 92: Richard Cranch and his wife, Mary, (Abigail's sister) had cared for Charles and Thomas while John and Abigial were abroad in the 1780s. William Cranch's appointment was to show appreciation.

CHAPTER TEN
p. 93: In one of his last acts as president, Adams had recalled John Quincy from Russia.

p. 93: John Quincy's election to the senate was especially sweet to his father because the opponent had been Timothy Pickering.

p. 95: A mastectomy is an excision or amputation of the breast.

p. 95: Anesthesia was not yet in common use.

p. 96: John Quincy had been recalled from Russia by President James Monroe to serve as Secretary of State.

p. 99: John Quincy Adams placed a marble tablet next to his father's tomb with the inscription: "On the Fourth of July, 1826, He was summoned To the Independence of Immortality And to the JUDGMENT OF HIS GOD."

Bibliography

Adams, Charles Francis, ed. *The Works of John Adams, Second President of the United States, Vols. VIII, IX, X*. Boston: Little, Brown and Company, Boston, 1854.

Bailyn, Bernard. *Faces of Revolution, Personalities and Themes in the Struggle for American Independence*. New York: Alfred A. Knopf, 1990.

Burnett, Edmund Cody. *The Continental Congress*. New York: W. W. Norton & Company, 1964.

Butterfield, L. H., ed. *Diary and Autobiography of John Adams, Vols. I, II, III*. Cambridge, MA: The Belknap Press of Harvard University Press, 1962.

————. *The Earliest Diary of John Adams*. Cambridge, MA: The Belknap Press of Harvard University Press, 1966.

Butterfield, L. H., Marc Friedlaender and Mary-Jo Kline, eds. *The Book of Abigail and John, Selected Letters of the Adams Family, 1762-1784*. Cambridge, MA: Harvard University Press, 1975.

Cappon, Lester J. *The Adams-Jefferson Letters, The Complete Correspondence Between Thomas Jefferson and Abigail and John Adams, Vols. I, II.* Chapel Hill: The University of North Carolina Press, 1959.

Chinard, Gilbert. *Honest John Adams.* Boston: Little, Brown and Company, 1933, 1961, 1964.

Commager, Henry Steele and Richard B. Morris, eds. *The Spirit of 'Seventy-Six, The Story of the American Revolution as Told by Participants.* New York: Harper & Row, 1958, 1967.

Ellis, Joseph J. *Passionate Sage.* New York: W. W. Norton & Company, 1993.

Ferling, John. *John Adams, A Life.* New York: Henry Holt and Company, 1992.

Fleming, Thomas. *Liberty! The American Revolution.* New York: Viking, 1997.

Haraszti, Zoltan. *John Adams, The Prophets of Progress.* Cambridge, MA: Harvard University Press, 1952.

Hofstadter, Richard. *The Idea of a Party System, The Rise of Legitimate Opposition in the United States, 1780-1840.* Berkeley and Los Angeles: University of California Press, 1969.

Morison, Samuel E. *The Oxford History of the American People, Vol. I.* 1965. Reprint, New York: Penguin Books, 1972.

Morris, Richard B. *Seven Who Shaped Our Destiny, The Founding Fathers as Revolutionaries*. New York: Harper & Row, 1973.

Peabody, James Bishop., ed. *John Adams, A Biography in His Own Words*. New York: Newsweek, Inc., 1973.

Russell, Francis. *Adams, An American Dynasty*. New York: American Heritage Publishing Co., Inc., 1976.

Schachner, Nathan. *The Founding Fathers*. New York: G. P. Putnam's Sons, 1954.

Shaw, Peter. *The Character of John Adams*. Chapel Hill: The University of North Carolina Press, 1976.

Shepherd, Jack. *The Adams Chronicles, Four Generations of Greatness*. Boston: Little, Brown and Company, 1975.

Smith, Page. *John Adams, Vols. I, II*. Westport, CT: Greenwood Press, 1969.

Withey, Lynne. *Dearest Friend: A Life of Abigail Adams*. New York: Free Press, 1981.

Wood, Gordon S. *The Creation of the American Republic, 1776-1787*. New York: W. W. Norton & Company, 1972.

Zobel, Hiller B. *The Boston Massacre*. New York: W. W. Norton, 1970.

Sources

CHAPTER ONE

p. 9, "Oh! . . . that I could . . ." Butterfield, L. H., ed. *Diary and Autobiography of John Adams. Vol. I, 7-8.* Cambridge, MA: The Belknap Press of Harvard University Press, 1962.

p. 11, "I cared not. . ." Peabody, James Bishop, ed. *John Adams, A Biography in His Own Words.* New York: Newsweek, Inc., 1973, p. 22.

p. 11, "What would you do . . ." Peabody, p. 23.

p. 11, "Be a Farmer." ibid.

p. 11, "A Farmer? Well I will . . ." ibid.

p. 12, "I like it very well." ibid.

p. 12, "Ay, but I don't . . ." ibid.

p. 12, ". . . the most indolent Man . . ." ibid.

p. 12, "Sir I don't like my Schoolmaster . . ." ibid.

p. 13, ". . . I had not the same confidence . . ." Peabody, p. 25.

p. 13, "Thinking that I must . . ." ibid.

p. 13, ". . .declared Admitted." ibid.

p. 14, ". . .perceived a growing Curiosity. . ." Peabody, p. 25-26.

p. 14, "Society of the Ladies." Peabody, p. 26.

p. 14, ". . . make a better Lawyer . . ." Peabody, p. 31.

p. 14, "I had no Money . . ." Peabody, p. 32.

p. 15, "a large number . . ." Peabody, p. 41.

p. 15, "I have no Books . . ." Butterfield, Vol. I, p. 22.

p. 15, "Dreamed away the Time." Butterfield, Vol. I, p. 38.

p. 15, "I am resolved . . ." Butterfield, Vol. I, p. 35.

p. 15, "Rose not till 7 o clock." ibid.

p. 16, "Yesterday I compleated a Contract..." Butterfield, Vol. I, pp. 42-43.

p. 16, "I set out with firm Resolutions..." Butterfield, Vol. I, p. 43.

CHAPTER TWO

p. 18, "I had no Acquaintance . . ." Butterfield, Vol. I, p. 54.

p. 18, "It is my Destiny . . ." Butterfield, Vol. I, p. 63.

p. 19, "It will be said . . ." Butterfield, Vol. I, p. 64.

p. 20, "My mind is liable to be called off..." Butterfield, Vol. I, p. 72.

p. 20, "If I look upon a Law Book..." Butterfield, L. H. ed. *The Earliest Diary of John Adams.* Cambridge, MA: The Belknap Press of Harvard University Press, 1966, p. 70.

p. 22, ". . . sitting with the Leggs [crossed] . . ." Peabody, p. 87.

p. 22, ". . . a gentleman has no business . . ." Peabody, p. 88.

p. 23, "O my dear Girl..." Butterfield, L. H., Marc Friedlaender and Mary-Jo Kline, eds. *The Book of Abigail and John, Selected Letters of the Adams Family, 1762-1784.* Cambridge, MA: Harvard University Press, 1975, p. 45.

p. 23, ". . . give [the bearer] as many Kisses..." Shepherd, Jack. *The Adams Chronicles, Four Generations of Greatness,* Boston: Little, Brown and Company, 1975, p. 19.

CHAPTER THREE

p. 28, "At Home, with my family." Butterfield, Vol. I, p. 270.

p. 28, "At Home. Thinking, reading..." Butterfield, Vol. I, p. 273.

p. 28, "The Year 1765 has been . . ." Butterfield, Vol. I, p. 263.

p. 28, "I have had Poverty . . ." Butterfield, Vol. I, p. 264-265.

p. 29, "It gave me much Pleasure..." Butterfield, Vol. I, p. 302.

p. 29, "The Choice was quite . . ." ibid.

p. 29, ". . . a place with fields . . ." Ferling, John . *John Adams, A Life*. New York: Henry Holt and Company, 1992, p. 56.

p. 29, "Am I grasping at Money . . ." Butterfield, Vol. I, p. 337.

p. 31, "a painfull Drudgery." Butterfield, Vol. I, p. 339.

p. 31, "This was always . . ." Peabody, p. 131.

p. 31, ". . . was the best entitled . . ." ibid.

p. 31, ". . . a sure introduction . . ." ibid.

p. 31, ". . . in an instant . . ." ibid.

p. 31, ". . . under any . . . Obligations of Gratitude . . ." Peabody, p. 132.

p. 32 "On my return I found . . ." Peabody, p. 115-116.

CHAPTER FOUR

p. 35, ". . . We were informed . . ." Peabody, p. 116-117.

p. 35, ". . . with their Musquets all shouldered . . ." Russell, Francis. *Adams, An American Dynasty*. New York: American Heritage Publishing, Co., Inc., 1976, p. 47.

p. 35, ". . . without taking the least notice . . ." ibid.

p. 36, ". . . Council ought to be the very last thing . . ." Peabody, p. 118.

p. 37, "I could scarce perceive . . ." Butterfield, Vol. III, p. 294.

p. 37, ". . . not guilty of murder . . ." Zobel, Hiller B. *The Boston Massacre*, New York: W. W. Norton, 1970, p. 294.

p. 38, ". . . one of the best Pieces of Service . . ." Butterfield, Vol. II, p. 79.

p. 38, "Farewell Politicks." Shepherd, p. 48.

p. 38, "Above all Things, I must avoid Politicks . . ." Ferling, p. 78.

p. 39, "Last Night 3 Cargoes of Bohea Tea . . ." Butterfield, Vol. II, p. 85.

p. 40, "This is the most magnificent . . ." Butterfield, Vol. II, pp. 85-86.

p. 40, "What Measures will the Ministry take . . ." Butterfield, Vol. II, p. 86.

p. 40, "The Buildings and the Water . . ." Butterfield, Vol. II, p. 88.

CHAPTER FIVE

p. 42, "an assembly of the wisest Men . . ." Butterfield, Vol. II, p. 96.

p. 42, "I feel myself unequal . . ." Butterfield, Vol. II, p. 96.

p. 42, "We have had Opportunities . . ." Butterfield, Friedlaender, Kline, p. 68.

p. 43, "When or where this Letter . . ." Butterfield, Friedlaender, Kline, 70.

p. 44, "This was one of the happiest . . ." Butterfield, Vol. II, pp. 134-35.

p. 44, ". . . amidst the Confusions . . ." Butterfield, Friedlaender, Kline, p. 77.

p. 44, "I long to return . . ." Butterfield, Friedlaender, Kline, p. 77.

p. 45, "It is not very likely . . ." Butterfield, Vol. II, p. 157.

p. 48, "Such is the Pride and Pomp . . ." Russell, p. 63.

p. 48, "My bursting Heart must find . . ." Peabody, p. 171.

p. 48, "It gives me more Pleasure . . ." Butterfield, Friedlaender, Kline, p. 96.

p. 49, "I almost am ready to faint . . ." Butterfield, Friedlaender, Kline, p. 108.

p. 49, "At this Distance . . ." Butterfield, Friedlaender, Kline, p. 109.

p. 49, "We have so much to do . . ." Butterfield, Friedlaender, Kline, p. 110.

p. 49, ". . . worn down with long . . ." Butterfield, Vol. II, p. 224.

CHAPTER SIX

p. 51, "We are in the very midst . . ." Commager, Henry Steele and Richard B. Morris, eds. *The Spirit of 'Seventy-Six, The Story of the American Revolution as Told by Participants.* New York: Harper & Row, 1967, p. 307.

p. 52, ". . . with a power of thought and expression . . ." Thomas Fleming, *Liberty! The American Revolution*, New York: Viking, 1997, p. 173.

p. 52, "the greatest question . . ." Commager and Morris, p. 320.

p. 52, "Our Affairs having taken a Turn . . ." Butterfield, Friedlaender, Kline, p. 161.

p. 52, "I suppose your Ladyship . . ." Butterfield, Friedlaender, Kline, p. 165.

p. 56, "I have many anxieties . . ." Butterfield, Friedlaender, Kline, p. 171.

p. 56, "My Mind is again Anxious . . ." Butterfield, Friedlaender, Kline, p. 178-80.

p. 56, "My Heart was much set . . ." Butterfield, Friedlaender, Kline, p. 182.

p. 56, "Is it not unaccountable . . ." Butterfield, Friedlaender, Kline, p. 184.

p. 57, "The Prospect is chilling . . ." Butterfield, Vol. II, p. 263.

p. 57, "Whether I shall be able . . ." Adams, Charles Francis, ed. *The Works of John Adams, Second President of the United States, Vol. IX.* Boston: Little, Brown and Company, 1854, p. 472.

p. 59, "Mr. Adams has given offense . . ." Russell, p. 89.

p. 60, "I must stay another Winter." Butterfield, Friedlaender, Kline, pp. 362-363.

p. 61, "I console myself . . ." Butterfield, Friedlaender, Kline, p. 375.

CHAPTER SEVEN

p. 62, "Your letter has made me . . ." Butterfield, Friedlaender, Kline, p. 391.

p. 63, ". . . [reluctant] . . . to leave behind . . ." Cappon, Lester J. *The Adams-Jefferson Letters, The Complete Correspondence Between Thomas Jefferson and Abigail and John Adams Vol. I.* Chapel Hill: The University of North Carolina Press, 1959, p. 14.

p. 64, "No step that I can take . . ." Shaw, Peter. *The Character of John Adams.* Chapel Hill: The University of North Carolina Press, 1976, p. 201.

p. 66, "To be explicit . . ." Butterfield, Vol. III, p. 211

p. 66, ". . . the [honorable] John Adams . . ." Butterfield, Vol. III, p. 211.

CHAPTER EIGHT

p. 69, "I have enjoyed a Luxury . . ."Cappon, Vol. I, p. 234.

p. 71, "My country has in its wisdom . . ." Shepherd, p. 157.

p. 71, "His Rotundity." Shaw, p. 230.

p. 71, ". . . sell Horses oxen Sheeps Cowes . . ." Shaw, p. 229.

p. 72, "I feel low-spirited . . ." Smith, Page. *John Adams Vol. II.* Westport, CT: Greenwood Press, Publishers, 1969, p. 807.

p. 74, ". . . powerfully operated to destroy . . ." Schachner, Nathan. *The Founding Fathers.* New York: G.P. Putnam's Sons, 1954, p. 126.

p. 74 "The history of our Revolution . . ." Smith, Vol. II, p. 802.

p. 74, ". . . something was . . . to be publicly said . . ." Smith, Vol. II, p. 815.

p. 76, ". . . who have endeavored to prepare . . ." Shepherd, p. 168.

p. 77, "I . . . am wearied to death . . ." Smith, Vol. II, p. 854.

p. 78, "I am heir apparent . . ." Smith, Vol. II, p. 880.

p. 78, "Either we must enter upon ardors . . ." Smith, Vol. II, p. 879.

CHAPTER NINE

p. 79, ". . . a dangerous crisis . . ." Peabody, p. 346.

p. 80, "A solemn scene it was . . ." Peabody, p. 358.

p. 81, "I must go to you or you must . . ." Shepherd, p. 184.

p. 81, ". . . a fresh attempt at negotiations." Ferling, p. 344.

p. 82, "George Washington had never . . . ." Shepherd, p. 190.

p. 82, "I wished in my heart it might have been . . ." Shepherd, pp. 190-91.

p. 84, "I will never send another . . ." Peabody, pp. 362-63.

p. 85, ". . . any libelous attack . . ." Shepherd, p. 197.

p. 86, ". . . sent by the Government of the United States . . ." Shepherd, p. 202.

p. 87, "I have . . . made up my mind . . ." Shepherd, p. 203.

p. 87, ". . . as readily as I could do . . ." Shepherd, p. 204.

p. 88, ". . . artful, designing men . . ." Ferling, p. 384.

p. 88, ". . . a Madman possessed . . ." Ferling, p. 386.

p. 89, "My children give me more Pain . . ." Ferling, p. 388.

p. 89, "I pray Heaven to bestow the best . . ." Smith, Vol. II, p. 1049.

p. 90, ". . . the melancholy death . . ." Shepherd, p. 210.

p. 90, ". . . unfit for the office . . ." Ellis, Joseph J. *Passionate Sage*. New York: W. W. Norton & Company, 1993, p. 22.

p. 90, ". . . I am confident . . ." Ellis, p. 23.

CHAPTER TEN

p. 93, "[Boredom], when it rains on a man . . ." Adams, Vol. IX, p. 585.

p. 95, "Why do you make so much ado about . . ." Adams, Vol. X, p. 12.

p. 95, ". . . many happy New Years . . ." Cappon, Vol. II, p. 290

p. 95, ". . . no circumstances have lessened . . ." Cappon, Vol. II, p. 292.

p. 96, "Every line from you exhilarates . . ." Cappon, Vol. II, p. 609.

p. 96, ". . . to close her days . . ." Chinard, Gilbert. *Honest John Adams*. Boston: Little, Brown and Company, 1964, p. 338.

p. 96, "My only daughter expired . . ." Cappon, Vol. II, p. 366.

p. 96, "quivering fingers" Ferling, p. 436.

p. 98, "The dear Partner of my Life . . ." Cappon, Vol. II, p. 529.

p. 98, "The multitude of my thoughts . . ." Adams, Vol. X, p. 416.

p. 99, "I am certainly very near the end . . ." Cappon, Vol. II, p. 613.

p. 99, "I will give you . . ." Peabody, p. 407.

p. 99, "Not a word." ibid.

p. 99, "Thomas Jefferson still survives." ibid.

Index